A Fireside Book
Published by Simon & Schuster
New York   London   Toronto   Sydney

THE ORGANIZED STUDENT

Teaching Children the Skills for Success in School and Beyond

DONNA GOLDBERG

WITH JENNIFER ZWIEBEL

FIRESIDE
Rockefeller Center
1230 Avenue of the Americas
New York, NY 10020

FIRESIDE and colophon are registered trademarks
of Simon & Schuster, Inc.

For information regarding special discounts for bulk purchases,
please contact Simon & Schuster Special Sales
at 1-800-456-6798 or business@simonandschuster.com

Designed by William Ruoto
Photographer: Saul Goldberg
Graphic artist: Ariel Camilo

Manufactured in the United States of America

11 13 15 17 19 20 18 16 14 12

Library of Congress Cataloging-in-Publication Data
Goldberg, Donna.
The organized student : teaching children the skills for success in
school and beyond / Donna Goldberg with Jennifer Zwiebel.
p. cm.
"A Fireside book."
Includes bibliographical references.
1. Home economics.   2. Orderliness.   3. Cognition in children.
4. Child development.   I. Zwiebel, Jennifer.   I. Title.
TX147.G615   2005
640—dc22   2005045051

ISBN-13: 978-0-7432-7020-5
ISBN-10:   0-7432-7020-7

For my boys, Jack, Noah, and Saul,
and
for Matt, my favorite teacher

ACKNOWLEDGMENTS

We would first like to thank our agent, Alice Martell, for believing in this project and for going above and beyond, every step of the way. Alice has served as guide, adviser, handholder, advocate, sample audience, cheering squad, and friend throughout this journey. She was there every time we picked up the phone and always had the right answer. This book would not be what it is (and may not have been at all) without her.

We would next like to thank Trish Todd at Touchstone Fireside for her excitement about and commitment to *The Organized Student*. Her insights were as invaluable as her patience with two first-time authors, and her feedback, as both parent and editor, helped shape this book. Trish gave new meaning to the concept of taking her work home with her, and for that we are grateful both to her and to her son, Mac, who let his mom practice organizing techniques on him. We would also like to extend our deepest gratitude to everyone else at Touchstone Fireside who helped make this production possible, particularly Mark Gompertz, Brett Valley, Martha Schwartz, Patricia Romanowsky, and Lisa Sciambra.

Many more people contributed to the birthing of this book. We would like to thank Terri Meyer, Sandy Greenberg, and Scott Frankel, who helped assemble a proposal that captured the heart and soul of our concept, for their highly trained eyes and extremely capable hands; Saul Goldberg, Elizabeth Camilo, and Ariel Camilo, who arranged, photographed, and edited the images used in this book, for their dedication and wonderfully perfectionist tendencies; and Heather Abel, Sarah Appleman, and Matti Feldman, who generously offered feedback on our writing, for helping this book move from concept to proposal to finished manuscript.

It goes without saying that this book could not have been written without the help of the wonderful, quirky, challenging, and insightful students we've worked with over the years; we thank them for all they have taught us. We would also like to thank our friends and family, who allowed us to be completely single-minded and ignore them while we were working on this manuscript.

And, finally, we would like to thank each other. In our pairing we found the inspiration, motivation, and capacity to achieve a dream. This was a once-in-a-lifetime opportunity and we are thrilled to have grabbed it with both hands.

Donna Goldberg

Thank you to my loving family: Jack, a great father and a role model of hard work, who gave me the space to evolve and mature and encouraged me to recognize my own abilities; Noah, the inspiration for The Organized Student, and living proof that organization can be the key to success; and Saul, who had his own battles to fight, who never gave up, and who found a path that has allowed him to flourish.

So many people have had a hand in helping me climb my mountains. I would like to take this opportunity to thank them. Dr. Clarice Kestenbaum, who first diagnosed my dyslexia and did more than help me: she saved me. She has always been my life raft, and it is because of her that I believe in myself. Audrey Zucker suggested that I become a librarian at Dalton, and Marilyn Moss embraced the idea. I learned from them what it meant to be a professional, and I will always be grateful to these two exceptional mentors. Marsha Kessler brought me into the world of learning disabilities as a colleague and has served as both guide and teacher. Joan Skurnick inspired me with a lecture and quickly became a much-valued adviser. Carol Saper planted the seed in my mind that the work I did with my son could be turned into a business. She lent me her own child to practice on and then went out and found me clients. Sue Appleman was always available as my business was getting started, whether acting as surrogate mom to my kids or as surrogate sister to me. She was (and is) the best friend one could hope for.

My NAPO colleagues have been a source of encouragement, inspiration, and guidance; thank you Sheila Delson, Barry Izsak, Linda Rothschild, and Stephanie Winston. I am indebted to all of the friends who have believed in me over the years, all extraordinary women who have seen me through the shifting landscapes of my life, particularly Cindi Becker, Marjorie Beutel, Jaclyn Braslow, Wendy Goldstein, Debra Hoffman, Carolyn Karp, Arlyne Landesman, Bunny Lederer, Leila Levitas, Beth Lowy, Linda Motelson, Sharon Oberfield, Laura Rabbitt, Joan Weberman, and Kate Whitney. I must also take this opportunity to thank Sylvia Quinagoran, who takes care of me while I'm busy taking care of everyone else.

And lastly, I am deeply grateful to my parents. They always believed in me. I wish they were here to see that their daughter, who couldn't read and struggled every day in school, has just written a book. They wouldn't be at all surprised.

Jennifer Zwiebel

My first thanks go to my parents, Goldie and Alan, and to my brother Louis, an original and eclectic group of teachers. Each has inspired me with his or her own brand of creativity, humor, and conviction. I thank my mother for her open heart and her unwavering faith in me, my father for his constant support and the pleasure he takes in my success, and my brother for his brilliant mind and generous spirit.

My next thanks go to doctors Susan Berg and Ron Hackett, who opened their home, shared their wisdom, and cooked for me while I was busy writing, and to Janine Davey, who provided both feedback and entertainment as needed. I could not have asked for a better second family.

I am incredibly grateful to all of the friends, colleagues, and clients who have shared so generously of their time, experience, and insight. I particularly want to thank: Natalie Blitt, for serving as a sounding board, offering excellent feedback, and always knowing when to tell me I'm doing a good job; Ilana Klein, for her passionate and vocal advocacy on my behalf and for her resounding faith in me; Adam Price, for his levelheaded and freely offered advice; Zehava Cohen, for always being willing and available to talk me through the process; Jessica Rutherford, for explaining the ins and outs of the business; Dr. Mary Campbell Gallagher, for providing innumerable resources and valuable suggestions; Dr. Jennifer Gerber and Dr. Adena Rosenthal, for their sympathetic ears and wonderful work; Dr. Laurie Weber, for opening a new window in my life and letting the air in; the entire Telushkin family, especially Dvorah, for her compassion and insight, Joseph, for his enthusiasm and counsel, and Benji, for his sense of humor and unique take on the world; and Norah Mazar Weglein, Alana Riss Fine, Ruby Gelman, and Rachel Perdue, for celebrating and commiserating with me, depending on the day.

Finally, I would like to thank my husband, Matt. He is, without a doubt, the smartest guy I know, and not just when it comes to comic books. His affinity for parallel structure, his passion for eliminating unnecessary commas, and his great love of language influenced the shape, flow, and feel of this book. His unstinting support enabled me to take on this project and see it through to the end, and his resounding faith in me shored me up when I was shaky. He is a treasure and I am so grateful to have found him.

CONTENTS

INTRODUCTION

Parenting is a humbling experience. You follow your instincts, do your best, and just when you think you're on the right track—the phone call comes. My phone call was from my son Noah's sixth-grade teacher, who informed me that my child hadn't handed in a single piece of homework all year. I was in shock. Noah spent hours in his room each night! And this was in the days before kids had computers in their rooms, which meant he wasn't instant messaging, playing games, or surfing the net. He didn't have a television or even a phone in his room. What could he be doing for hours on end? I felt like a terrible mother—why hadn't I asked to see his homework? Why didn't I know how he spent his time? And why wasn't he handing anything in?!

It turned out that Noah was, in fact, doing his homework. Upon investigation, I found nearly a semester's worth of completed, ungraded assignments buried in the dark recesses of his backpack. This made absolutely no sense to me. Why would someone go through the trouble of doing his homework and then not hand it in? Thus began my journey into the world of the disorganized student.

Disorganization was unfamiliar territory to me. My problems in school stemmed from a different set of challenges. I didn't learn to read until I was in the sixth grade. When I was little I would cry in my cubby every day before school; when I got older I dreaded the failure I knew awaited me in the classroom. I became a master at looking like I was paying attention when in fact I was in a completely different universe. I didn't want anyone to know how stupid I was, so I did my best to make myself disappear in class and I prayed that teachers wouldn't call on me so I wouldn't embarrass myself in front of my classmates. Unfortunately, I didn't know how to turn off the disappearing act at the end of the school day. A few years ago a former classmate recognized me in a bookstore. "Oh, Donna," she cried. "I remember you! You were so sweet and so nice, but you were always sort of . . . invisible."

Life is painful for students who don't meet the expectations of their parents, teachers, and peers. Some kids suffer from learning issues and others from disorganization. Whatever the obstacle, its effects are devastating to a child's self-esteem. I survived in school for two reasons. First, I had a mother who was nonjudgmental and accepting, who stood up for me and was available whenever I needed her. When she recognized that she wasn't equipped to handle my challenges alone, she sought help from professionals. In the days when there was no such thing as a learning specialist, she found tutors to help me learn to read. Her tenacity became my model when it was time for me to help my own kids. Second, I was extremely organized. I developed excellent organizational skills as a way to maintain some control over the things I was being taught but didn't understand. Being organized not only helped me get through school and adjust to living with dyslexia before it was a known diagnosis, but it also enabled me to become a school librarian and put me in the position to help other students succeed in school.

When I received the phone call from Noah's teacher I realized how different a student Noah was than I. I had always assumed everyone knew how to be organized, and now I was seeing for the first time that it wasn't true. Noah's backpack weighed more than he did and made him look like he was better equipped for a cross-country trek than a crosstown bus ride to school. His homework got done and often managed to make it into his backpack, but that was where the train derailed: his assignments never saw the light of day again. At the age of eleven, Noah was missing deadlines, constantly searching for school supplies, running late between classes, and, as a result, starting to fail some of his subjects.

When I recognized that one reason Noah never handed anything in was because he couldn't find anything in his backpack, I began to make connections between Noah's organizing habits and his academic performance. Once I understood the effects of his behavior, we worked out a system that enabled him not only to keep track of his homework but also to make sure he handed it in.

As a middle school librarian I knew that Noah wasn't the only one having trouble keeping track of his things. Each May I would chase down library books that were taken out in October. The kids who had taken them out always had the best intentions and plenty of excuses: "I'll bring it in tomorrow," "It's somewhere in my room," "I swear it was in my locker last week!" I soon realized that these were the same students who began to have trouble in sixth grade when school became departmentalized and they were faced with multiple classrooms and teachers. Their names came up in faculty meetings year after year as the symptoms they had exhibited early on with their overdue library books now manifested themselves in overdue assignments, missed homework, and deteriorating grades. The root of the problem had nothing to do with the students' intelligence or motivation to do well in school; it had to do with their lack of basic organizational skills.

I began applying some of the lessons I learned with Noah to the students in the middle school library. I helped them come up with ways to keep track of their paper and taught them how to meet deadlines. I developed theories about students and organization and used my friends' kids as guinea pigs. The students I worked with began to find success in school, and in 1990 The Organized Student was born. As a professional organizer I was able to help students from middle school through graduate school learn techniques that allowed them to work more effectively and increase their productivity. Word of mouth helped my business grow quickly, and in 1997 I left my position as a librarian to become a full-time consultant.

I've worked with hundreds of students and have certainly learned as much from them as they have from me. In the past few years I've noticed changes—an increase in pressure on students, heavier workloads, and an overwhelming number of distractions—that have made it more important than ever that students have strong organizational skills. I wrote this book to share what I've learned with as many students as possible, and I wrote it for those who are closest to children and who are most invested in seeing them succeed—their parents.

It's important to keep in mind that school today is not the place it was when you were growing up. Students have substantially more work, their days are more fragmented, and there's a pervasive sense of pressure leading students to feel that they can't afford to make mistakes. Advances in technology, overloaded schedules, and changes in family structure mean students are facing a different and often overwhelming world.

Entering middle school has always been challenging. When classes become departmentalized, children suddenly find themselves responsible for organizing their time and setting their own priorities. Over the past two decades the home computer and other technologies have made life even more overwhelming for students (as well as adults). Middle and high school students are drowning in paper, inundated with handouts, printouts, and packets. They lose hours each day to e-mail, instant messaging, and the Internet. The number of distractions available to students has increased exponentially, and their academic performance is suffering because of it. Without some training in how to handle the new paper flow, workload, and schedule, a student is lost.

In addition to these academic challenges, children today

face new and often complex situations at home. In many households, both parents work outside the home and are unable to supervise their children as closely as they would like. Children of divorced parents may divide their time between two homes, and many families are headed by single parents or guardians. Even if there are two parents at home the students themselves are often not. Extracurricular activities take up precious hours of a student's study time; she may not arrive home until late in the evening, leaving barely enough time to eat dinner and complete her homework. If she's already struggling in school, having to search for the right notebook or call friends for the assignment may be one step too many.

If you and your child invest the time it takes to organize supplies, homework, and a study schedule, you can create the structure that he needs to succeed. While this book offers many different strategies and systems for getting organized, they will work only if you communicate openly with your child without being critical. Everyone learns differently and each student will come up with his own "right answers." It's vital that you recognize the importance of maintaining a nonjudgmental attitude and that you address each situation with an open mind, a positive approach, and no eye rolling. The fastest way to end an organizing session with your child is to criticize him. Keep your eye on the long-term goal and don't get distracted by a failed test or a notebook full of doodles. When you learn to stay focused and listen for the problems, you will discover that a solution can always be worked out.

Keep your ears open and your mouth closed—you never know what seemingly insignificant detail will turn out to be the key to understanding what your child needs.

Learning to be organized is a process. It requires dedication, a little optimism, and a lot of support. It's a skill that needs to be taught, practiced, and honed, and there isn't a child (or adult) who can't benefit from the lessons in this book. Use the Assessment Questions provided in each chapter to pinpoint the places in your child's academic life where the system breaks down and discover insightful ways to rebuild each element, from the backpack to the bedroom. There are countless ways to make things fun and efficient, and as many unique solutions as there are students.

In this book I offer the tricks and tools I've gathered over the years, many of which came from the wonderful students with whom I've worked. You've taken the first step towards helping your child create an organized life. With time, patience, and the desire to help, you can teach your child invaluable lifelong skills. I wish you the best of luck as you embark upon this journey.

CHAPTER 1

Understanding the Organized Student

There are two types of organization: cerebral and physical. Cerebral organization allows you to organize information mentally, filing it in your brain so that you can access it, manipulate it, and use it to generate new ideas. Physical organization refers to the way you manage your space and your stuff. This book explores the aspect of cerebral organization that relates to time management and addresses physical organization and how it impacts academic achievement. By examining your child's habits and academic patterns, you will be able to determine where he's running into trouble. Once you understand the nature of the difficulty, you can design solutions that match his needs.

Is My Child Disorganized?

In order to create an organized student, you need to know what one looks like. The rule of thumb is that an organized

student can find what he needs when he needs it. More specifically, an organized student:

- Doesn't carry everything he owns in his backpack
- Can identify and bring home the books, supplies, and
  worksheets he needs in order to complete his homework
- Can locate his finished homework in class and hand it in
  on time
- Can study efficiently because he knows when tests
  are coming up, has set aside enough time to study,
  and doesn't waste time looking for class notes and
  handouts

The disorganized child, on the other hand, exhibits a
range of behavior that inhibits his performance in school. Be-
havioral patterns signaling disorganization emerge at different stages of development. Some students show signs of
disorganization at an early age, while others are fine until middle school or high school when everything suddenly falls
apart. Some indications of disorganization in younger children include maintaining a messy school cubby and having
trouble making it from one room to the next without losing
something. Older students' patterns are even clearer and more
problematic. The disorganized student:

- Frequently loses papers
- Doesn't hand in assignments on time or at all
- Has a backpack full of crumpled paper and random
  objects

- Can't break down long-term projects and misses deadlines
- Leaves everything for the last minute
- Disrupts home life with frantic searches, urgent requests for late-night help, and anxiety-ridden meltdowns

School performance is affected not only because the disorganized student can't meet deadlines or find his homework but also because he counts any time he spends doing anything related to school as study time. This means that the forty-five minutes spent searching for history notes counts as forty-five minutes of studying—and of course he deserves a break after "working" so hard.

It's also likely that the disorganized child's bedroom is a disaster area, although a cluttered bedroom is not always a sign of a disorganized child. Being messy and being disorganized are two different things. You may not be able to see the floor in your child's bedroom, but if he can find what he needs and hands his work in on time, if he is prepared for tests and gets good grades, disorganization is probably not an issue. His room may be a wreck, but there's an underlying structure that enables him to function, even if it's not apparent to you. On the other hand, if a child has a chaotic bedroom and is exhibiting signs of academic distress, it's likely that disorganization is contributing to the problem.

What's Not Being Taught in School

A student's ability to locate his class notes, bring home the right textbook, and complete and deliver an assignment on time is just as vital to his success in school as his ability to read or write. The concepts and practice of organization and time management, therefore, need to be a part of every school's curriculum. Basic skills, like decoding and addition, become assumed abilities in middle school and teachers build on them. When a student doesn't grasp the fundamentals in a particular area, he quickly falls behind. As his classmates move on to the next level, he can't follow. The same is true with organizational skills. He'll have a hard time focusing on a lesson if he's busy searching for his notebook, just as he will find it challenging to compare and contrast two books if he has difficulty grasping the main idea of a story. Like the student who has trouble with reading comprehension, the disorganized child will fall further and further behind until he gets help.

Many educators and parents have learned to recognize deficiencies in reading, writing, and math, but not in organization. Instead of being looked upon as a set of skills that needs to be taught, organization is seen as something instinctive, something everyone should be capable of. *While some students do have the innate ability to organize themselves, many don't.* Because we don't attend to students who exhibit problems in this area as we do students who have trouble with math or reading, the disorganized student rarely gets the help he needs. The gap in his education continues to grow and has an increasingly negative impact on his academic career.

Younger children are provided with some organizational guidance in school, but the lessons end before many students can absorb them. Between the second and fourth grades, teachers spend a lot of time creating structure and organization in their classrooms. They set up well-defined procedures that serve as cues for staying organized and they model behavior for students. What they *don't* do is explain *why* they are doing what they're doing. This makes it difficult for students to adopt these behaviors as their own. Teachers count on students to pick up on visual clues and to mimic their behavior, and students who are not visual learners or who do not draw connections to the bigger picture are left without an important set of skills. In later years when these students fail to live up to their teachers' expectations, they are told to try harder or to stop being lazy. Rather than acknowledging a deficiency in a student's education, we accuse him of having a character flaw.

When everyone buys into the image of the lazy or hopelessly disorganized student, it only reinforces the student's behavior and the belief that nothing can be done. There are, of course, parents and educators who recognize a need and try to help. What generally happens, however, is that an adult tries to impose her own ideas about organizing on a student, even if the ideas are not suited to the child's particular learning style. A student may learn better visually than verbally or think alphabetically and not by color. The point of this book is to help you understand what your child's needs are so that you can develop solutions that work with his learning style.

LEARNING STYLES

The term "learning style" refers to the way in which a person usually perceives, organizes, and recalls information.
Most people tend to be stronger in one particular modality.
Once you determine which learning style works best for your child, you can tailor your lessons to his strengths. The ideal lesson incorporates all three modalities.

■ **Visual** learners rely on what they can observe. They are particularly receptive to written information, such as class notes, textbooks, charts, diagrams, and pictures. They often recall information by remembering where it was located on a page or by associating it with an image. *If your child is a visual learner, color and sequence will play a large role in his organizing systems, and he will learn by watching what you do.*

■ **Auditory** learners take in information by listening. Methods of learning that work well for them include hearing class lectures, reading their notes out loud, and teaching others. *It's important to talk through each part of the organizing process with your child if he is an auditory learner. Explain what you're doing, why you're doing it, and how he should use each tool.*

■ **Kinesthetic** learners absorb by doing. They process information through touch and movement. They learn best when they write things down, act out concepts, and construct models. They also learn well from demonstrations. *If your child is a kinesthetic learner, organizing needs to be a hands-on process. Let your child assemble and manipulate the tools and show you how he plans to use them.*

Organized Teachers, Disorganized Kids

While younger children tend to be kept in line by school rules and watchful eyes, many students fall apart as soon as teachers stop setting up classroom structures. A number of years ago I was lecturing to a group of parents and teachers at a local school. In between talks I observed classes so I could offer feedback to the faculty and administration. The fourth-grade class was led by an extremely well organized teacher. At the beginning of the year she had set up a mailbox system in which each student was assigned a cubby. Every day she would place the students' homework, worksheets, and permission slips in the mailboxes and the students would collect them at the end of the day. Towards the end of class I watched the children retrieve their homework, pack up, and prepare to go home. As the teacher reviewed each sheet that the students should have received, Stuart called out that he was missing his math worksheet. The teacher checked the mailbox—it was empty. She had the other students look through their backpacks to make sure no one had taken the homework sheet by accident. No one had.

In the meantime, Stuart was busy dumping the contents of his backpack onto his desk. I wasn't surprised as the crumpled papers, worn notebooks, and old snacks spilled out, but I did a double-take when a pair of RollerBlades emerged. How could Stuart possibly find *anything* he needed with those RollerBlades taking up so much space?!

The state of the backpack set off warning bells immediately; I knew that it probably signaled a larger pattern of disorganization. I guessed that this was not the first time Stuart had misplaced his homework, and I had a feeling I could pick out his cubby by looking for the messiest one in the room. In the meantime, there was still no worksheet, and now the school buses were being held up to wait for Stuart's classmates while they searched the room. Finally, his teacher found the homework—it had slipped under Stuart's desk—and the class was dismissed.

After the classroom emptied I spoke with Stuart's teacher and learned that my instincts had been correct: the worksheet incident was not an isolated one, Stuart consistently lost his homework or left it at home, and his cubby was a disaster. The teacher knew that Stuart was disorganized and had mentioned her concerns to his parents, but because he did well academically, his organizational issues were put on the back burner. She tried to make sure that his homework made it home each night, but beyond that she didn't know what she could do.

I walked out of that classroom knowing two things: one, Stuart needed to find a new way to carry his RollerBlades, and two, he was going to run into serious trouble when he hit middle school. As soon as classes became departmentalized and teachers no longer micromanaged every step, Stuart would not be able to sustain any systems on his own. While his current teacher had wonderful organizational skills, she had not taught them to Stuart. She didn't explain why something was being implemented or how it worked, and she didn't break the systems down or let students discover how to organize for themselves. Without someone guiding him through every step of the process, Stuart was destined to miss a lot more than a worksheet.

ANALYSIS

■ Students who don't have innate organizational skills don't internalize the structures teachers set up in the classroom. Stuart's teacher devised a great way to handle paper flow, but she never explained its purpose or demonstrated how she came up with the solution. Because Stuart didn't understand either the concept of organizing paper or the method behind the system he could not repeat the process independently.

■ Stuart's teacher micromanaged the classroom but was unable to help Stuart manage the clutter that pervaded his life. Stuart's backpack and cubby needed to be purged, and someone needed to explain to him that carrying around so many things was making it harder for him to find what he needed.

■ Children exhibit telltale signs in early childhood that point to a tendency towards disorganization. These signs are not always academic; it may be that your child often loses things or that papers and toys seem to magically disappear between one room and another; it may be that permission slips never make it home or that at parent-teacher conferences you can immediately identify your child's desk because it's the messiest one.

Warning: Transitions Ahead

By the end of fourth grade, teachers assume that students have an understanding of basic organizational skills. However, when students leave their homerooms and begin to change classrooms throughout the day and the focus shifts from process (how to do things) to product (finished work), many students get lost. Teachers become subject-specific, and instruction is focused on individual areas of study rather than on the general skills students need to survive in school.

Even students who had no academic difficulty in elementary school can easily fall apart in middle school. As a school librarian I could spot the lower-school kids who were likely to run into trouble when teachers' expectations changed without warning. They were the kids who always came to the library last to choose books for their reports and either couldn't pick a topic or picked something so esoteric there were no books on the subject. They focused on the more obvious goal of the assignment (to learn about ancient Egypt, for example) and did not infer the other significant goal, which was to learn how to write a research paper. The teacher wanted to impart the *process* to her students. She wanted to teach them how to find proper research materials, create note cards, devise an outline, write a first draft, and then edit it into a final paper. She wanted them to learn how to break down long-term projects and set and meet deadlines. These are the building blocks students have to master so that they can later focus on critical thinking and textual analysis. Students who miss the implied lesson are unable to use these foundational skills as they continue their education. Every time they have to write a paper, they must relearn the entire process. These are the kids who are going to be left behind as school progresses.

When students like these are faced with multiple subjects, teachers, and classrooms, the survival systems they've used to get themselves through school so far can quickly disintegrate. Suddenly they are expected to transport loose paper, notebooks, and textbooks for every subject between classrooms, locker, and home. They are responsible for handing in homework unsolicited and for breaking down long-term projects over weeks or months, even though they have never learned how to do these things on their own. They are exhausted by the effort they put into trying to keep themselves together and by the extra work they have to do every time they have to make up an assignment. They often end up doing twice the work more organized students do and by the end of the school year they're completely drained.

In order to stop these students from falling through the cracks, we must be able to recognize the telltale signs of disorganization that can lead to problems in middle school. If educators and parents learn to identify the signs, students can be helped sooner and be better prepared for what lies ahead.

Explosive Evenings and Other Symptoms

A student's habits and behavior have far-reaching consequences. They affect not only her grades and self-esteem; they also affect her family. Natalie had been getting A's and B's throughout elementary school, but once she hit sixth grade her grades dropped to C's and D's. Her twin sister wasn't having trouble with the transition into middle school and Natalie was starting to act out. Her MO was to do her homework all over the house which, of course, often led to missing assignments and frantic last-minute searches. At 10:30 one night Natalie desperately tore the house apart looking for the homework she had been working on all evening. Her anxiety threw the whole family into chaos. Frustrated and exhausted, Natalie lashed out at her parents and blamed them for moving her work. An explosive fight ensued that left everyone drained and miserable.

The next morning Natalie's father woke up still fuming about the previous night's fiasco. He asked Natalie again and again whether or not she had found her homework. After ignoring the question as long as possible she suddenly "remembered" that she had actually done her homework in school and left it in her locker. Her dad, annoyed and suspicious of the changing story, decided, against Natalie's rather vocal protests, to drive her to school and investigate for himself. Standing in the school hallway, he watched in amazement as several sweaters, a tennis racquet, three cans of tennis balls, heaps of paper, and a pile of textbooks with uncracked spines tumbled out of Natalie's locker. The homework, needless to say, was not there. They called me the next day.

Natalie had been an A student when she didn't have to multitask, but keeping track of several classrooms, teachers, and subjects was difficult for her, both physically and mentally. Her papers, notebooks, and textbooks were all over the place. It was hard to switch her focus from math to history when she was busy trying to find her classroom and locate the notebook she was supposed to be writing in. She was also having a hard time adapting to different teachers' personalities and expectations; she was so busy trying to figure out what everyone wanted, she barely had time to focus on her work.

Given enough time, Natalie would likely have adjusted to the changes in school on her own, but she would have missed so much academically that she would have been playing catch-up for the rest of the year. As it was, she couldn't hand in assignments because she either lost them or hadn't written them down in the first place. She couldn't keep up with class reading because she couldn't find the books she needed to bring home, and she wasn't doing well on tests because she didn't know when they were and didn't have any notes to study from. Natalie was a smart kid who wouldn't be having academic difficulties were it not for her organizational problems.

Our goal was to organize the technical aspects of Natalie's academic life so that she could focus on *doing* her work instead of on *locating* it. Before our first meeting I had instructed Natalie to empty the contents of her locker into shopping bags and bring them home. We sorted through the bags together to get an accurate picture of how many textbooks she was dealing with and to determine whether a binder might work better for her than carrying seven separate notebooks. We created a filing system so she could clear out old notes and handouts once a unit was completed instead of carrying a year's worth of papers in her backpack.

We then set up a planner, giving Natalie one place to record all of her assignments and an opportunity to see the bigger picture. We recorded deadlines and test dates using her class syllabi, and I encouraged her to articulate what she already knew about her teachers' different personalities and expectations. Soon Natalie was able to discern some of her teachers' patterns: one teacher gave quizzes every Friday; another always collected homework on Tuesdays; some were strict about deadlines and binder checks, while others were more lenient. The more Natalie could pinpoint and predict her teachers' habits, the more she could concentrate on her schoolwork. When we talked it through she was able to frame her teachers and classes in a context she understood. This helped ease her anxiety about school.

Over the course of the next several months we tweaked the systems until Natalie felt comfortable with them. They certainly didn't all fall into place at once (she struggled with paper flow, and for several months we continued to find paper everywhere), but the planner changed her life immediately. Just knowing what to do and when to do it made her an achiever again. Once she felt in control of her life she was able to focus her energy on studying; soon her grades went back up to A's and B's. Natalie's ability to keep track of her homework also greatly reduced the tension at home. With the positive family dynamic restored, everyone could actually laugh when Natalie found the missing homework under her parents' bed, three months after she'd finished it on their bedroom floor.

ANALYSIS

■ Late-night meltdowns tend to come at the end of a long school day (and at the end of a long workday for parents). Everyone's exhausted and patience is often in short supply; tension escalates quicker than you can blink.

■ Natalie's frustration was not a result of challenging academics, it came from the difficulty she had making transitions in school. Many students have a hard time making transitions from year to year, and if it doesn't all go smoothly it's almost impossible for them to focus on what they're supposed to be learning in class. How can you be searching for your notebook and listening to the teacher at the same time? How can you show up late to class and expect to catch the whole lesson? Anxiety over transitions and change can interfere with a student's ability to listen and learn.

■ When you take away the anxiety over nonacademic issues, your child will be able to focus on learning. Systems for maintaining paper flow and tracking assignments, as well as an organized backpack and locker, put the control back in your child's hands. A sense of continuity throughout the systems you create together will allow her to do the best work she is capable of doing.

Looking Ahead to High School

Organizing Natalie put her back in control and allowed her to focus on schoolwork. But what she experienced in the transition from lower school to middle school might well be echoed in a few years when she enters high school. High school is another great leap for students. They are suddenly faced with even more requirements, choices, and changes. The level of individual responsibility and accountability is raised, and not all students are equipped to handle it. Even if you have already addressed your child's organizational issues, you may have to intervene again. Some kids learn the systems once and continue to modify them to meet their needs. Others might take a few steps back when they begin high school and may need some review. If this is the case, you and your child can tweak her systems in order to accommodate her new schedule and course load. If you understand that this might happen, you won't be thrown if it does. With a good foundation and solid skills your child will simply need a few adjustments and a little encouragement as she moves on to the next stage in her life.

When Is It More Than Disorganization?

Physical organization and time management play a large part in every student's ability to succeed in school, but sometimes a student needs support beyond paper-flow and time-tracking systems. Executive function, often referred to as "the brain's CEO," describes the brain's ability to perform several different tasks in order to achieve a goal. Some of the specific tasks include a person's ability to:

- Understand the concept of cause and effect, perceive potential consequences, and inhibit behavior accordingly
- Sequence, categorize, and prioritize
- Stay focused on a task
- Make smooth and timely transitions from one subject or activity to another
- Manipulate information to answer questions about familiar material posed in an unfamiliar manner and to generate new ideas
- Apply one lesson in a similar situation instead of relearning the lesson each time
- Hold on to new information while you're using it (called "working memory")

When someone experiences trouble with these skills *(executive dysfunction),* he will have difficulty with organization and planning. The visible clues will be typical of a disorganized student, but you may also see symptoms in a student's ability to process information, make transitions in school or at home, behave appropriately in social situations (by not interrupting others or changing the topic of conversation), or foresee consequences and act accordingly. The systems in this book are a good foundation for any student, and particularly for those who experience executive dysfunction. If your child demonstrates significant difficulty in these areas, however, you should consult a qualified professional. Together you can identify the specific areas your child is struggling with and determine the best approach to helping him.

Keep in mind that children develop at different rates. While some students who exhibit signs of executive dysfunction early on will need to learn to compensate for the skills they lack, others will eventually mature and acquire the skills they're missing. Also remember that today's fast-paced, high-tech, hyperscheduled world demands that children develop executive function skills earlier than ever before.

In my work with students I have come across children who are physically disorganized, others who are cerebrally disorganized, and still others who share signs of both types of disorganization. While getting organized will not resolve problems posed by such challenges as learning disabilities or emotional issues, it will help put control back in your child's hands, which is the first key to unlocking his potential.

CHAPTER 2

Getting Started: The Journey Ahead

Anthony was a seventh grader who, according to his teachers, wasn't performing up to his academic potential. He was a charming young man who was involved in his school newspaper and served as the sports statistician for his basketball team. He was smart enough to do grade-level work, but he wasn't handing in his assignments on time or bringing home the proper study materials, and his papers were all over the place.

One of the first things I discovered at our initial meeting was that Anthony did his homework on the floor. When I asked him why he didn't work at his desk, his answer was very matter-of-fact: "There's no room to work and there's nothing in the drawers that I need." He was absolutely right. The desk was cluttered with CDs, magazines, computer games, and baseball paraphernalia. While it was not our first priority, eventually the time came to address his desk, and as we emptied the drawers onto the floor we unearthed his entire collection of baseball cards. We dumped all of the cards into a large garbage bag and set them aside so that we could stay focused on the task at hand. At the end of our session I told Anthony to ask his mom to pick up some storage boxes so his card collection could be put away properly, and we stowed the bag in his closet.

We met regularly over the next few months to work on academic organizing. Sometime towards the end of the school year, I recalled the baseball card collection and asked Anthony what had happened to it. He informed me that the cards were now conveniently stored all over his closet floor. Apparently the storage boxes never made it home. Like most parents today, his mom's days were crammed and her lists were long; this task simply fell through the cracks. The garbage bag stayed in the closet until it broke and the cards spilled out.

I arrived at our next session with two large plastic bins. As we stacked the cards in the bins, I turned to Anthony. "This is a no-brainer! You could easily do this with your mom!"

Anthony rolled his eyes. "Yeah, right. If I sat down with my mom to try and do this, it would go like this: my mom would start, 'Anthony, if you spent as much time on your schoolwork as you do on your baseball cards you'd be an A student!' Then I'd get mad and say something to her, then she'd get mad, the phone would ring, she'd get up to answer it, and by then we'd both be so fed up and angry, the cards would stay on the floor."

Working with your own child is tricky. The act of organizing a collection of baseball cards should be simply that—an act, not a battle. When parents make these tasks personal, they become negative experiences to be dreaded and avoided. Kids learn to hate organizing and cleaning and become more resistant to working with us. At the age of thirteen Anthony had already developed a distinct communication pattern with his mother. Even a conversation completely unrelated to school reverted to his academic performance and then escalated into an argument. Sound familiar? As you go through this organizing process, continually remind yourself of your goal. Is this the time to introduce some basic principles of organizing or to discuss school? Is your goal to help your child put away his baseball cards or to argue about grades? Thinking about your motivation will help you stay on track and prevent benign interactions from becoming explosive fights.

How to Approach Your Child

When I work with students I have the advantage of being an outsider. Kids are generally well behaved and willing to listen to what I have to say. Your child will likely be less polite with you and will not give you much time to explain what you're trying to accomplish. This chapter, in addition to taking you through the structure of the book and providing guidelines for implementing the lessons, will offer tips on getting the most out of working with your child. You've both had years to discover what sets each other off and you'll both do it automatically when you become frustrated. One way to avoid such conflicts and work productively is to view the organizing process as a business venture. The language I employ throughout this book ("session," "appointment," "project") reinforces a less personal and more businesslike arrangement;

it draws new boundaries and sets up a different dynamic between you and your child. If you can put your regular parenting style on the shelf for a little while and maintain a semiprofessional distance from your child, the time you spend together organizing will run more smoothly.

There is no question that some children are easier to raise than others. Some kids will follow your lead without hesitation, and others will fight you every step of the way. Some will persevere until they get the results they want, and others will throw up their hands at the first sign of defeat. There is also no question that some parents will find this process more challenging than others. Parents who don't have innate organizational skills needn't worry; this book is designed to take you step-by-step through the process. In fact, parents who are highly organized themselves may have more difficulty pulling back and letting their children make decisions. You are going to have to discover your child's individual learning style and encourage her to come up with her own solutions.

If you want these interactions with your child to be productive, you can't be the mom or dad she is expecting you to be. You're going to have to make some changes in the way you approach her, and probably in the way you think about her as well. The better you understand your child and her needs, the better you can help her, and the better you can teach her how to help herself.

The Three-Part World of the Organized Student

The organized student's world consists of three main areas:

- Organization in school
- Organization at home
- Time management

This book examines these specific areas of a student's life, demonstrates how a student's systems tend to fall apart, and then offers solutions that will help set her on the track to success.

ORGANIZATION IN SCHOOL

Your child needs a place to keep current class notes and handouts, a way to get everything from home to school and from classroom to classroom, and someplace to store everything when she's not using it. The binder/accordion file, the backpack, and the locker are the three storage systems that can make your child's school day more efficient and productive. When she can find what she needs when she needs it—whether it's textbooks, school supplies, sports equipment, computer games, or lunch—her anxiety in school will be reduced and she will be able to focus on learning.

ORGANIZATION AT HOME

Your child needs a place to do her homework and an easy way to store papers and projects she isn't using in school anymore. She also needs to be able to function both in her bedroom and within the household at large. The Desktop File Box, your child's desk, and the Portable Office are tools that make doing work at home less stressful and more effective. This book will also provide practical ways to make your child's room work and offer tips for keeping shared space under control.

TIME MANAGEMENT

Although this chapter comes towards the end of the book, it is one of the most pivotal steps in the organizing process. Time management encompasses everything from gauging how long an activity will take to mapping out a realistic schedule for completing assignments on time. The tool I use to teach students about time and accountability is a customizable plan book in which students record homework and extracurricular activities and keep track of long-term assignments. It corresponds to a student's binder and desktop files in both color and sequence and helps students learn to plan, prioritize, and manage their time. Long-term and household schedules emphasize the importance of planning within a larger context.

How to Begin

You will need a certain amount of information at your fingertips before you begin to help your child organize. Read a chapter, make some action notes for yourself, and gather information by answering the Assessment Questions. This will enable you to formulate some ideas before you approach your child so that she might actually believe you know what you're talking about.

I generally have a two- to three-hour window of opportunity to capture a student's interest, devise a plan, and execute it. You, on the other hand, have time on your side. Take advantage of this luxury and introduce new pieces of the puzzle as your child is ready. You should be able to complete the initial Paper Flow and Time Management setup within a ten-day period. Start by reading the chapters about Paper Flow (chapters 3 through 5) and answering the Assessment Questions. Use your child's feedback to determine which supplies you

A WORD ABOUT ASSESSMENTS

The aim of the assessment is to raise your consciousness of what it's like to be a student and, in particular, what it's like to be your child. Each set of questions should be an eye-opening experience. It probably has never occurred to you to ask your child these questions. They won't give you all the answers you need or present a fully formed solution, but they will certainly give you an understanding of how your child's day works, what her requirements are, and what systems are or are not already in place. They will not tell you what your child is studying, but they will give you a picture of what kind of student she is. With an understanding of all of the factors that go into your child's day (and not just the academic elements), you'll have a better chance of making her a more organized and efficient student.

will need and keep track of everything on The Organized Student Supply List at the back of the book (this way you can make just one trip to the store). Gather your supplies and decide on a time to meet.

Your first session should run between one and three hours and cover the locker and backpack, a Traveling Paper System, and the Desktop Filing System. The amount of time this will take depends partly on where your child is in the school year (the earlier in the year, the less paper you will have to sort through). The second session, which will focus on the Desk or Portable Office (chapter 6), should also take between one and three hours, depending on the current state of your child's desk. The third session revolves around Time Management and the Planner (chapters 7 and 8) and should take between forty-five minutes and an hour and a half. Of course, everyone works differently, and you need to find a pace that suits your child. When your child empties her backpack on the living room floor, take a look at the pile of paper in front of you and plan your time accordingly. The bedroom, if you are planning to address it, can take anywhere from a few hours to several days, depending on how much needs to get done and which areas you're going to work on.

Block off the amount of time indicated for each part of the process and be clear with your child about your plan so you don't get into arguments later. Say something like, "We're both doing this for the first time, and I don't know how long it's going to take. Let's block off two hours. If we finish early, great. If we don't finish within two hours, let's take a break and finish it later in the day."

Before you begin, talk to your child about the purpose and process of organizing. Explain that you're interested in helping her organize her schoolwork, introduce the three components of The Organized Student (home, school, and time), and point out the effect organization can have on her ability to succeed in school. Present an overview of what you'll be doing together and give her concrete reasons that show her why this process is important to both of you (these skills will allow her to become more independent; you won't be on her back all the time to get her work done; there will be less tension at home). Emphasize the fact that these are skills you use every day in your own life, and, because they are not taught in school, you want to teach them to her.

Finally, explain to your child that you expect to make adjustments along the way. This way you will both have realistic expectations, and, perhaps more important, you will be taking responsibility for the system's success or failure off your child's shoulders. Children who are having difficulty in school already expect to fail; if you can alleviate your child's fear she will be more likely to give the process a chance instead of giving up at the first sign of trouble. When she recognizes that having these basic skills will allow her to adapt as life changes, she will become both more confident and more independent.

Follow Through

The downside to your having complete access to your child is that it will be much easier for you to nag her than it is for me. Don't. Maintaining some distance will give you a chance to see how your child handles everything. She may engage you in conversation about how well everything's working or how nothing's working at all. Respond briefly: "That's great!" or "Let's look at it on the weekend and see how we can sort it out." If your child is really in distress, you can address the situation right away, but remain calm—two anxious people don't solve problems.

Your child may not say anything, and that's okay too. Don't hound her with questions or push for details. Don't ask her every day if she feels better or if the system is working. If it's not working, ask her to be specific—"*Nothing's* working!" is not helpful feedback. Ask, "What exactly isn't working? Are you having a hard time finding your papers? Is it hard to write down your homework because you have to dig your planner out of your bag?" It's up to you to figure out where your child is getting stuck, and you can do this by asking questions, looking at the systems, or speaking to her teacher. If her systems *are* working, don't take it as an invitation to add to what she's already doing. Let her enjoy her success and wait until your next appointment to move forward.

I schedule a follow-up appointment two weeks after I first work with a student in order to give her time to use her new systems. At the follow-up appointment I can see what worked and what didn't work, and we can adjust the systems accordingly. After you and your child set up the complete organizing system, including both paper flow and the planner, you should walk away for a couple of weeks. When you meet for a follow-up session, see how things are working, tweak the systems, and encourage your child to keep going. Three weeks to a month later, meet again. This is not a weekly appointment but a periodic check-in. By this time, some kids' systems will have started to fall apart, which is completely natural. Others will be holding up, but at some point papers will start to stray, a homework assignment will be missed, and your child will become less vigilant about maintaining her systems. It's not unlike buying a new car—you're thrilled to own it, you're enamored of the new car smell and the impeccable finish. Then you get your first dent and the honeymoon is over. You let the tissues and water bottles gather in the backseat and pretty soon it doesn't feel like a new car anymore. But a car is there to be used, as are a backpack and a binder; there's no point in trying to keep any of them in pristine condition.

Encourage your child to use her new systems consistently. Don't wait too long for a follow-up appointment; most kids can maintain their systems for three to four weeks. If you wait much longer the system runs the risk of falling apart and you will be starting from scratch, most likely with a suspicious (and antagonistic) child.

Getting Results

Kids like to see immediate results. When you start by setting up a paper flow system, your child can see results the next day. She should start to feel much more in control after the entire system is in place—handing in assignments and bringing home the right books, finding what she needs in her backpack, and being able to locate all of her class notes. Parents often sense a difference right away as well. When I return for a follow-up visit, I often learn that the tension around the house has been greatly reduced.

I stay away from a student's desk and bedroom until a student is comfortable with me, and I stay away completely if the state of her bedroom is not affecting her grades. If your child is fighting the organizing process, focus on the academics and delay working on the desk or bedroom. Put it off as long as you need to, even if it means ignoring the desk for the rest of the school year. Work on the more pressing issues. You can address behavior that effects the household at large, such as shared space and extracurricular schedules, but closing the door to your child's bedroom may be the best solution in the short run. As long as nothing is living in the bedroom that shouldn't be, a kid can live in a pigsty if she's getting straight A's. And keep in mind that if your child is disorganized there's a good chance that she doesn't care about being messy; don't waste your one shot to grab her attention by working on something that doesn't matter to her.

Meeting Resistance

This is a process, not an event. It will involve a lot of trial and error, adjustments and regular maintenance. There will be good days and bad days. Once in a while everything will fall apart and you and your child will have to put it all back together. Don't worry; it's par for the course—and be sure to tell this to your child. Eventually she will be able to navigate the organizational waters on her own. Until then, you're in this together.

Keep in mind that every child works differently. Your child may want to take on the whole project at once or be able to handle only one small piece at a time. She may take to the new systems right away or be uncomfortable with change and take longer to adjust. She might be able to maintain everything herself or need to review the process with you until it becomes her own. Whatever your child's style, make sure you work at a pace that's comfortable for her.

Most children who are truly disorganized will not be able to change their behavior in several areas at once. Focus on one area at a time and encourage your child to work on the tools that are easier for her to manage. Some students will start using the planner immediately but continue to struggle with paper. Some will keep their new binders in perfect order but resist writing down their homework. Just stay with it and continue to reinforce the system until your child feels she can rely on it. Success breeds success; when your child sees results from one part of the system, she should be ready to move on to the next.

Also keep in mind that your child may not be ready to start this process when you are. She may think she's doing fine in school and may not want your help. Forcing your child to get organized against her will is only going to turn her off to the idea altogether. While no kid is going to immediately embrace the prospect of organizing her notebooks when she could be chatting with her friends online, most do become engaged when they see new school supplies. From there you can usually move forward. If your child isn't ready to do this it will be pretty clear that she's blowing you off. About half an hour into the session, if your child refuses to participate, is not engaged, or has tried to pick six fights with you, then it's time to back off.

Say to her, "This is not a good time to work on this. Let's try it another day."

At some point an opportunity to reintroduce the idea will present itself. It may be after she's thrown the entire house into chaos by starting a

> **THINK ABOUT IT**
>
> Don't set the systems up yourself. If your child hasn't created her own solutions, they won't really suit her needs, and if she's not invested in the systems she won't maintain them.

ten-page research paper the night before it's due or when she gets her grades back after the first marking period and she's failed three out of five subjects. Don't reintroduce the idea of organizing while you're gripping the report card in your hand, and don't be punitive ("I told you so" never goes over well with kids). Wait a couple of days for things to calm down and then say, "I know your grades were as disappointing to you as they were to us. I think we should give getting organized a shot. It certainly won't hurt and it may help improve your grades." Grab the chance to be positive and take action.

Remember that this is not about what *you* need or what works for *you*. You may have amazing organizing skills, but that doesn't mean your systems will work for your child; she is not you and she doesn't solve problems the way you do. Explain to your child that you're both entering new territory and that it's going to take some trial and error. If something that worked yesterday isn't working today, that doesn't mean it's not a good solution. Don't be too quick to abandon what you started and look for something new. Kids have the tendency to do that. Instead, give the systems some time and a lot of reinforcement, and both you and your child will benefit from the long-term results.

The Nitty Gritty

Working successfully with your child depends largely on how you introduce the process to her. You're going to have to prove that you can be trusted, stay focused, refrain from criticizing, and really help make her life better. It's no small order, but there are several ways in which you can prepare for a successful partnership.

- **Explain the process to your child in a positive light.** Children who have trouble in the classroom, whether it's because of learning issues or organizational problems, feel like failures. This is your golden opportunity to explain to your child that she's not stupid, that in fact school has changed and teachers' expectations have changed. Acknowledge that she's going to have to adjust the way she works in order to succeed in this new environment, but she doesn't yet have the skills she needs to do so because *they were never taught to her*. Explain that you will be creating systems and tools together that will help her find her way.

- **Set yourself up for success.** Approach your child when you know she'll be most receptive to the idea of working together on this project. Don't bring up the notion of organizing her backpack first thing in the morning if you know all you'll get in return is a growl.

- **Remove temptation.** Tell your child to put away anything she doesn't want you to see before you work together. It will be easier for you to refrain from getting upset or critical if you don't find failed tests or late assignments. This is not a permanent ban—feel free to get on her back about the grades tomorrow—just stay focused on the task at hand today.

- **Sign a contract.** You may want to go as far as signing a contract that states something to the effect of, "I promise not to go ballistic, and if I do we'll stop the session. You promise to give me the time necessary to complete your academic setup." If you do make this promise, however, you have to keep your word.

- **Hand over control.** Do whatever you can to help your child own the process. Let her pick a time to work together and encourage her to ask questions and make suggestions along the way. She can also choose supplies she likes, assemble the tools herself, use a label maker or write out her own labels, and make decisions about how she wants her systems to look.

- **Limit distractions.** Make a point of avoiding phone calls and interruptions from other family members while you're working with your child. Turn off your phone and let the answering machine pick up. Choose a time when

THINK ABOUT IT

At the end of the day, the system your child chooses isn't nearly as important as her ability to maintain it. When an adult experiences difficulties with time management, she will likely go out and buy every calendar under the sun. She will quickly find herself swimming in PDAs (personal digital assistants), computer programs, wall calendars, desk calendars, and daily planners. The tendency is to try one system, hit a bump in the road, toss the system, and try a new one.

This pattern will go on indefinitely because the belief that "this will be the one to organize my life" will never bear fruit. The answer, for both adults and children, lies not in the particular system but in whether it's used consistently. Whether your child chooses a binder or an accordion file, regular use and maintenance will make the difference.

no one else is around, or put someone else in charge during your organizing session.

- **Put a sock in your mouth.** In general, the less you say, the better. If you can refrain from commenting on all the things you think your child "should" be doing differently and give her a chance to discover things for herself, you have a great shot at creating something that works. When I work with students, I let them label their own binders and files. Inevitably the labels go on crooked (which makes me crazy), but I'd rather have a kid involved in the process and feeling good about what she's accomplishing than an immaculate binder that goes unused.

- **Always give positive feedback.** Be careful not to focus on what *hasn't* been accomplished. The best way to foster success is to praise your child's achievements and couch criticism in positive terms. For example, "You're really being consistent about writing all your homework down! I see you have a long-term assignment. Why don't we try breaking it down together and putting it in your planner?" or "You're doing such a great job getting all your papers home. I see a couple of loose papers floating around in your backpack—I guess the day must have been hectic. Why don't you take a minute and put them away?"

The Long Haul

Your child will take her cues from you. If you can maintain a relaxed attitude about the process, she will feel comfortable experimenting. Let her know that the systems you come up with together may or may not work, but you're in it for the long haul. If something doesn't work the first time it just means you haven't hit upon all of the answers yet. Emphasize the fact that it's not *her* failure. There are enough things going wrong in your child's academic life that she doesn't need to add organizing to the list. Once the technical aspect of organizing becomes second nature to a student, she will be able to focus on what she needs to learn as opposed to focusing on finding her textbook and figuring out what chapter to read. And as you work towards this goal, you will be developing another equally important set of skills—your child's ability to make her own choices and discoveries.

CHAPTER 3

Lessons from the Black Hole: The Locker and the Backpack

It's amazing how many things disappear into the seemingly bottomless depths of your child's locker and backpack. On the last day of school (or the last day of summer) when the backpack is unceremoniously dumped out, it's not unusual to discover the missing book report, science project, or permission slip that caused so much grief earlier in the year. This chapter explores the two black holes in a student's life—the locker and the backpack—and shows you how to use them to help identify the roots of your child's organizational issues. It will then help you and your child lay the foundation for his organizational overhaul. Remember, this book is designed to teach you the skills you need to guide your child along the road to success, but you have to let *him* drive the truck. The systems that work will be the ones he has invested in personally.

It is important that you understand what your child experiences on a day-to-day basis so that you can begin the organizing process on common ground. Imagine you're a student. You're carrying a portable office on your back all day, holding everything you need for all of your subjects. Every forty-five minutes, six times a day, five days a week, you have to pack and unpack your books, binders, notebooks, planner, pens, pencils, calculator, graph paper, protractor, dictionary, and anything else you need for a given class. To dig out what you want from your backpack, you have to burrow through several CDs, your cell phone, candy wrappers, the sweatshirt you meant to leave at home, and layers of loose papers that never made it into a folder. You have between two and five minutes to make a mad dash from one classroom to the next (usually on another floor, if not in another building altogether), sometimes sprinting to your locker first, where you have to dig through your gym clothes, more CDs, an old science project, leftover snacks, and a pile of textbooks in order to find what you need for class. After repeating this scenario six times, you have to figure out what to bring home for homework, pack it up, get it home, spread it out, do your work (assuming you know what it is), or call several friends to get your assignments, and then get it all done, put it away, and start all over again in the morning.

There's no chance that you won't lose, misplace, or break something at some point. By the time you've been in school for a month you will have packed and unpacked your backpack close to three hundred times. By winter break you will have gone through the process nearly fourteen hundred times. You're also carrying around a load of old worksheets, printouts, tests, quizzes, and handouts—a couple of hundred sheets of paper that you're too afraid to take out of your backpack because you think you might need one of them again in class. Feel a little overwhelmed? Your child feels like this *all the time*. He may have had trouble when he was assigned to *one* classroom and *one* teacher. Now he's in unfamiliar territory, switching rooms and switching teachers and feeling completely out of control—and he has no idea how to handle it.

Assessment: Understanding Your Child's Day

This is your first set of Assessment Questions. Remember that this is an information-gathering tool, not a shortcut to a solution. The aim of these questions is to help you get a sense of what your child's day is like so that you can help him come up with systems that make sense. You can answer some of these questions simply by observation; others will require the assistance of your child or someone in your child's school. Use the answers provided or supply your own, depending on your child's situation. In some instances you may find that a single question requires multiple answers. Answer what you can and ask your child the rest of the questions later, preferably in one sitting. Try to engage him in the process by saying something like, "I've been reading this book about getting organized and it talks about how different school is today than when I was growing up. I'm blown away by how much harder it is for you!" or "I wouldn't have thought to ask some of these questions—they really made me think about how difficult school can be." Try to catch your child at a moment when he can focus on what you're saying, whether it's at the dinner table or (my personal favorite) in the car with the doors locked.

To give you a realistic sense of how much time your child actually has to manage himself and his belongings in school

- *How much time is there between the end of one class and the beginning of the next?*

- *How long does it take your child to get from one class to another?*
  a. Are the classes on the same floor?
  b. Does he have to travel from one end of the building to another?
  c. Does he have to switch floors?
  d. Does he have to switch buildings?
  e. Is he allowed to use an elevator or does he always use stairs?
  f. Are there specific classes in which the teacher lets your child out late or doesn't give the class time to pack up?

- *Where is your child's locker located?*
  a. Convenient to all of his classes
  b. Convenient to some of his classes
  c. Near homeroom
  d. Near nothing

To help you and your child determine the most logical and efficient way to organize his locker and backpack

- *What is your child's schedule like?*
    a. He has the same classes in the same order every day.
    b. The order of his classes changes every day.
    c. The school runs on a five-day schedule (every Monday to Friday remain the same every week).
    d. The school runs on a rotating schedule that changes from week to week.
    e. Other: _____.

- *What extracurricular activities does your child participate in, and what supplies or equipment does he need for them?*

- *Does your child keep his supplies and equipment in a locker at school, or do they travel back and forth between school and home on a regular basis?*

- *How many books is your child required to keep track of throughout the day? (I worked with a student in dual-language school who had twenty-two books!)*

- *Would it be helpful to keep a second set of textbooks at home?*

- *Does your child's school offer second sets of textbooks on loan?*

- *What unique situations is your child experiencing this year? For example, the school is under renovation and classes are being held in a trailer, or the school ran out of lockers and your child has to share with someone who keeps changing the lock.*

Now you can begin to make some choices. If, for example, your child's class schedule is consistent throughout the week, he can separate the contents of his locker into two sections, morning and afternoon. This way he can go back to his locker just once during the day to exchange the textbooks and notebooks he uses for his morning classes for those he'll need in the afternoon. If, on the other hand, his schedule changes every day, he'll probably want to divide his belongings differently. He may want to keep textbooks together on one shelf and notebooks on another, or keep all materials pertaining to specific classes together.

Based on his schedule and the location of his locker, your child may want to start planning ahead, taking enough materials with him to last until the next time he can get back to his locker. If he has two minutes between classes, he's not going to have time to run back to his locker for a workbook, and if his locker is on the first floor and all of his classes are on the sixth, he's not going to want to make the trek more than once a day.

The First Black Hole: The Locker

Sue's mother contacted me in June to set up an appointment for the following school year. Panicked, she told me that her daughter was so disorganized that by the end of seventh grade she wasn't handing in assignments and was constantly losing things. Sue was also coping with some hearing loss, visual processing issues, and dysgraphia (a neurological disorder that results in barely legible handwriting). Sue's mom was herself very organized and had tried creating a color-coded system for Sue, but it didn't help. It sounded like Sue was struggling with several learning issues that were affecting her performance in school.

When we met for the first time, I was sure Sue's mom had her pegged. Although I had asked Sue to bring all her belongings home from school, she brought home only the book she needed for homework that night. I also learned that she was upset about a permission slip she was supposed to hand in but had already managed to lose. Old patterns were back and it was only the first day of school; we needed to make some changes quickly, before Sue became defeated and shut down.

The first thing we had to do was collect all of Sue's school supplies and books. When I asked Sue how close her school was, her face turned white. Recognizing one of the signs of teenage panic, I told her not to worry; if we bumped into anyone she could tell them I was a family friend visiting from out of town and she was giving me a tour of her school. Relief washed over her face and we headed out the door. When we opened Sue's locker I saw that the extra shelf her mother had given her to separate her books was sitting uselessly at the bottom of the locker. It quickly became clear why: you needed a hammer to get the shelf into place and Sue didn't happen to have one lying around. It took our combined strength, plus my shoe, to knock the shelf into place. As we banged away, a slip of paper floated down from behind the top shelf. Sue picked it up and discovered, to her relief, the permission slip she thought she had lost; it had been in her locker the entire time.

The shelf, in theory, was not a bad idea, and Sue's mom was well-intentioned, but it was unrealistic to expect Sue to hunt down a hammer or take off her shoe in the middle of the hallway and bang the shelf into place. Without some adult supervision the shelf would have stayed on the bottom of her locker all year. Once the shelf was in place we were able to organize Sue's locker. Her schedule happened to be consistent throughout the week (she had the same classes in the same order every day) so we designated one shelf in her locker for morning classes and one for afternoon classes.

At the end of the day I was delighted by this student whom I had expected to find so challenging. It turned out that many of her "issues" and academic difficulties were a result of her physical disorganization. When her setup changed, she became an academic star. I saw her only once more—she was one of the rare students who experience a major turnaround and hardly need any more help. Her mother was able to help her maintain the systems we had put in place and Sue's confidence soared for the rest of the year.

ANALYSIS

■ Be realistic about teenagers. The locker shelf was a good idea, but if Sue's mom wanted to make sure it was actually being used, she had to follow up. A week into school she could ask Sue if the shelf was installed and if the answer was "no," they could work out a plan to get it done.

■ Sue was dealing with several challenges. Changing her physical setup helped tremendously, but her learning issues would require ongoing professional intervention and support.

■ Sue's mom had wonderful organizational skills, but when she tried to help her daughter nothing seemed to stick. There were a couple of reasons why Sue was able to get organized with me:

■ **The tools made sense.** I offered Sue several options so that she could create a cohesive system that made sense to her. When her mom worked with Sue, she set up systems without asking for Sue's input. The systems didn't match Sue's learning style and she wasn't invested in the outcome.

■ **I used different modalities.** If Sue didn't understand what I was saying (auditory), she could learn by watching what we were doing (visual) and by assembling things herself (kinesthetic).

Assessment: The Locker

The following questions are designed to give you a sense of the physical layout of your child's school and a picture of her schedule and routine. The process of organizing the locker is intertwined with the process of organizing the backpack.

Answer the questions below together with the second set of assessment questions on pages 55–56, and you'll be better equipped to tackle both.

- *What does your child keep in her locker?*
    a. Textbooks and notebooks

    b. Extra school supplies

    c. Athletic equipment

    d. Mirror, makeup, and hair spray

    e. Snacks

    f. Everything she needs—but she can't find anything

    g. Nothing (she hasn't opened it since the first day of school)

- *What is the condition of the locker?*
    a. It's well organized.

    b. It's a disaster area.

    c. Sometimes it's all right and sometimes it's a mess.

    d. She can't get it open.

    e. She's afraid to get it open.

    f. She can't get it closed.

- *What type of storage and accessories does your child's locker already contain?*
    a. A shelf or shelves

    b. Hook(s)

    c. A narrow locker with a separate wide section above

    d. Other: _____

- *What additional accessories does your child think would be helpful?*

- *Is your child to go back to her locker between classes?*

- *Does your child have time to go back to her locker between classes?*

- *Does your child have a top locker or a bottom locker?*

- *Does your child share a locker?*

- *Does your child have a lock on her locker and if so does she remember the combination and know how to use it?*

Action: The Locker

This is your first opportunity to organize with your child. If you don't want it to be your last, remember rule number one: *accent only the positive*. Keep negative feedback to yourself. Save it for another time if you have to. If you find you're too upset by what you see or what you find, stop and walk away. Excuse yourself and don't let your child know how upset you are. You can say something like, "I'm feeling a bit overwhelmed. I can't focus right now—let's come back to this later." You've got one shot to start the process, and no kid is going to work well while he's being criticized. Holding back is definitely one of the most difficult things to do as a parent, but it is absolutely necessary if you want to help your child succeed.

Also keep in mind that this process will go more smoothly

with some kids than with others. You know your child better than anyone else does. He may be willing to work with you and take everything one step at a time. He may give you one shot to pull together the entire system, and if you blow it you're out of luck. He may work with you only under threat of punishment or promise of reward. Whatever you have to do, take the commitment seriously and keep your focus on the task at hand. Success, whether it's an organized backpack or an hour spent together without arguing, will bring your child back for session number two.

HOW LONG WILL THIS TAKE?

The locker and backpack should be addressed at the beginning of the first session. It may take fifteen minutes, it may take three times as long. When the locker and backpack have been sorted and reassembled, you can move on to creating a Traveling Paper System and a Desktop File Box. If your child is overloaded with paper and organizing the locker and backpack takes longer than you anticipated, don't worry about the next stage. Get the locker and backpack up and running and continue the process another day.

When you're starting the session come armed with as much knowledge as possible. After answering the assessment questions use the PACK method, described below, to help your child reorganize his locker. You can begin this process with your child whenever you are both ready—in September, before school starts, or in May, before finals. It's never too late to get organized!

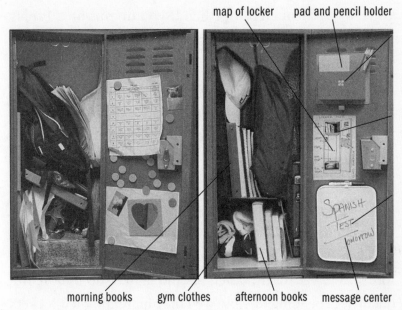

map of locker   pad and pencil holder

morning books   gym clothes   afternoon books   message center

The locker: before and after.

PACK
(Purge, Accessorize, Categorize, and Keep It Up!)

PURGE

- This step can either be done in school or at home. If your child plans to do this in school, he can use the floor as his workspace for purging and organizing. Most kids, however, will not want to do this in school with their friends around. They also may not be able to do it alone—and they will almost certainly not want you joining them at their lockers. If this is the case, send your child to school with shopping bags, a duffel bag, or a large, strong garbage bag and tell him to bring everything home so that you can go through it together. If you do this on a Friday you should be able to find an hour over the course of the weekend to work on it.

- After you *ask permission* to view the contents of the bags, throw out anything your child doesn't need (old food, papers your child can't decipher, fliers for events that have already taken place).

- Purging, which is different from regular maintenance, needs to take place a few times a year. Set a schedule with your child to do a regular, thorough clean-out. Some students will only need to do this two or three times, usually right before school vacations; others should plan to do it more frequently, depending on how well they maintain their lockers once they're set up. Most students can do the maintenance alone in school; they won't have to bring home the contents of their lockers again unless the school requires it.

ACCESSORIZE

- **Find out what your child needs access to: books, binders, gym bag, etc.** He probably won't be able to tell you in the first week of school, but within a couple of weeks he should have a sense of what he uses on a regular basis. His needs may change over the course of the year (new classes may be introduced, sports seasons will change), so discuss what needs to be accessible each time your child purges his locker.

- **Outfit the locker with accessories** that make it easier for your child to find things. Extra hooks, an additional shelf, a mirror, and a stash of extra pens are some good options. Let him be creative, but remind him that whatever he comes up with should move him towards the goal of keeping his locker organized. You can show him a list of accessories and let him choose the ones he thinks he'll actually use:

- Extra shelf
- Copy of schedule
- Message center
- Pencil holder with extra pens and pencils
- Basket for gym clothes
- Map of locker
- Mirror
- Batteries
- A few dollars (hidden) in case he forgets his lunch money

- **Follow up** by asking your child if everything's been installed in his locker or if he needs some help. Obviously you won't know exactly how it's working unless you visit the school (which is something I don't particularly recommend), but a gentle reminder may be the nudge he needs to get the job done.

CATEGORIZE

- **Separate the contents of the locker into categories:** textbooks, notebooks, loose papers; clothing; gym bag, sports equipment; musical instruments, art supplies, and other extracurricular accessories; anything else your child needs in school on a regular basis.
- **Have your child sort through the loose papers.** Anything that no longer belongs in school can be kept at home and

filed in the desktop file box (see chapter 5, "Where Paper Lives at Home"). Papers that are still being used in class or that pertain to the unit your child is currently studying should be stored in the appropriate place in your child's backpack (chapter 4, "Traveling Paper").

- **Subdivide** textbooks and notebooks by subject or by morning and afternoon classes, depending on your child's schedule.

- **Avoid doing the same job twice.** Don't sort everything at home and then throw it back in a single bag—your child will have to sort everything again when he gets to school. Pack up what he's going to be taking back to school in separate bags according to category. For example, the contents of each locker shelf should be placed in a separate bag. You can send an additional bag of items that go back in the locker however they fit most easily (gym clothes, extra school supplies). Place the smaller individual bags in a single large bag so your child has only one item to carry. When your child gets to school he can simply empty the contents of each bag into the designated section of the locker.

KEEP IT UP

- **Show your child that there are plenty of things in your life that get out of control** if they're not regularly maintained (try using your briefcase, handbag, stack of mail, or laundry hamper as an example). Explain what regular maintenance means (getting rid of garbage, consistently returning items to their proper place), and let him make the connection to maintaining his locker.

- **Explain to your child that his locker will get messy again** within a few days, a week, or a month, and that's to be expected. However, if he assigns all of his belongings a home and makes an effort to put things back where they belong, it will be easier for him to find what he needs when he needs it.

- **Create a "map" of the locker** indicating where everything is stored. Draw an outline of the locker with its different components (shelves, hooks, door, etc.) and use arrows to show what's kept where. This will make it easier for your child to reassemble the locker when it starts to fall apart.

- **Even if he doesn't put things back consistently,** he may begin to associate items with their designated spots in the locker and then start to establish a sense of predictability. The locker is a good place to practice creating and maintaining a personal space because it's small, contained, and easier to manage than a bedroom.

The Second Black Hole: The Backpack

Some kids will clean out their backpacks in ten minutes and be left with a small stack of papers that need to be filed. Others will have stray papers all over the place and need to invest a lot more time organizing their backpacks and everything that comes out of them. I worked with Jack, a high school junior, in late February. When I asked him to empty his backpack I quickly found myself ankle-deep in paper. We spent the next three hours on the floor sorting through handouts, worksheets, homework, tests, quizzes, and class notes. Somewhere toward the end of the first session I realized that Jack had been carrying around every piece of paper he'd received since the first day of school.

It's not unusual to find several months' worth of papers in a student's backpack. He may carry everything around because he thinks he might need his papers in class, he's afraid to lose his work, he has no time to deal with sorting and storing old papers, or because he has nowhere to put them once they come out of his backpack. This is normal. The Paper Flow System you assemble with your child will address each of these issues.

What concerns me more than the student who is flooded with paper is the student who has no paper at all. If your child comes home with an empty backpack, you need to find out where he's keeping his paper. It's possible that his school uses a portfolio-based system, which means that your child's teachers hold on to a lot of his schoolwork. But if you discover that there is no paper in your child's backpack, locker, bedroom, or school, you have an issue that needs to be dealt with. At least the student with a backpack crammed full of paper is present in school—he's taking notes, collecting handouts, and doing work. The student with the empty notebook and folders is lost. Something isn't clicking cerebrally. He doesn't understand the structure of what he's learning, which makes it hard to take notes and complete assignments. He can't determine what's important and what's not, and he doesn't understand that he'll need to access information again for tests and papers, so he throws everything away. This is not about organization. It's a serious issue that may reflect learning difficulties, such as comprehension or language processing issues, or emotional stress. Whatever is impairing a student's ability to succeed in school needs to be addressed by a trained professional so that appropriate steps can be taken.

Assessment: The Backpack

These Assessment Questions will help you and your child develop a convenient and orderly way to transport everything your child needs in school.

To help gauge what you're dealing with

- *What do you see when you look at your child's backpack?*
    - a. A place for everything and everything in its place
    - b. Loose paper everywhere
    - c. Folders crammed full of random papers
    - d. As many accessories that don't relate to school as do— CDs, video games, makeup, baseball cards
    - e. Something that you would only approach with extreme caution and a pair of rubber gloves

To help determine how to approach your child

- *How would your child feel if you looked through his backpack?*

    a. He wouldn't care.

    b. He would flip out.

    c. I wouldn't think of touching it without asking permission.

    d. What difference does it make? I'm doing this to help him!

- *How does your child use his backpack in school, and what are the school regulations?*

    a. He is allowed to carry a backpack in school all day.

    b. He is not allowed to use his backpack in school and must carry loose books and papers from class to class.

    c. He returns to his locker between classes to exchange his books.

    d. At lunchtime he switches books from his morning classes with books for his afternoon classes.

    e. He carries everything with him all day.

    f. He brings everything home in his backpack just in case.

- *Your child's backpack weighs _____.*

THINK ABOUT IT

This is a good time to explore the relationship you have with your child vis-à-vis personal belongings and privacy. Think about your child's attitude to your belongings—is he allowed to dig around freely in your purse or wallet, does he need permission or is it simply never done in your home?

binder or accordion file

books placed in size order

The backpack: before and after.

Action: The Backpack

Use the PACK method to address the contents of your child's backpack. It follows the same structure as the locker-organizing system but addresses the specific elements of the backpack.

PACK
(Purge, Accessorize, Categorize, and Keep It Up!)

PURGE

- **Clear enough space** on the bedroom floor or kitchen table to spread out.
- **Have a large garbage pail** or trash bag within reach.
- **Remove everything from the backpack** and lay it out on the cleared surface.

- **Throw out** things that are obviously garbage, such as candy wrappers and papers that are crumpled beyond recognition.

- **Isolate the things your child doesn't need** to carry in his backpack anymore. Let him come up with the answers. It may be a book he's no longer reading in class, returned assignments and tests that will not be reviewed again in school, or a sweater that could use a good washing. Put them in a pile so that they can be put away later.

ACCESSORIZE

- **Make a list of accessories** that will make it easier for your child to find what he's looking for. Some options include a pencil case, a cell phone holder, a bus pass holder, and a keychain that attaches to the backpack.

- **Fill out a luggage tag** or use a copy of the form below and attach it to your child's backpack in case it gets lost. (Note that on the sample form the student's home address is not included in case your child carries house keys in his backpack.)

- **A word of caution** about water bottles: if the top pops up, your child's backpack will be completely waterlogged. I'm speaking from personal experience. Keep the water bottle on the outside of the backpack (many backpacks have pockets specifically designed for water bottles), or use a different type of bottle and make sure your child keeps it separate from his books and papers.

GENERAL INFORMATION

Name: _____

Telephone: _____ Cell: _____

School: _____

School Address: _____

PARENTS' WORK NUMBERS:

Mother: _____ Cell: _____

Father: _____ Cell: _____

EMERGENCY INFORMATION:

In case of emergency notify: _____

Telephone: _____ Cell: _____

MEDICAL INFORMATION:

Physician: _____ Telephone: _____

Allergies: _____ Blood-type: _____

IF LOST — PLEASE RETURN — REWARD

Sample form to be attached to your child's backpack.

CATEGORIZE

- **Separate** everything else that came out of the backpack into piles: textbooks, notebooks, loose paper, homework planner, materials for extracurricular activities, music and games, and any other category that presents itself.
- **Ask your child to identify the books he needs** for that night's homework. Keep in mind that the disorganized child often tries to bring home *all* of his books in order to cover his bases. Unfortunately, because he can't really tell

what's in his backpack, he often ends up bringing home everything but the one thing he actually needs. If your child has brought home textbooks he doesn't need or that don't belong to him, *let him realize it*. Have him make two piles, one of books he needs that night and another of books that can be brought back to school, left at home, or returned to friends.

- **Have your child gather and sort** all loose papers by subject. Current papers should be stored in the appropriate section of your child's binder or accordion file (see chapter 4, "Traveling Paper").

- **Have your child return his textbooks, binders, and folders to the backpack.** If he puts things in randomly help him see that he'll have a hard time finding what he's looking for. If he stuffs his copy of *The Great Gatsby* in between his calculus and history textbooks he'll never be able to find it. If he arranges his books and binders in size order, however, everything will be easier to locate (and he won't have to make up pretend quotes in class).

- **If your child's backpack has multiple sections,** assign everything a home. This will help him learn to put things back in the same place on a regular basis. Even if he doesn't do it every day (and in the beginning he won't) he will know where things belong and once a week he can reorganize his backpack. Eventually he'll know where to look for something when he needs it.

- **Create a "map" of the backpack** on an index card that shows what items go in which section. Tack it to your child's bulletin board or file it in his desktop file box. It

THINK ABOUT IT

If your child doesn't seem to know how to tell which textbooks to bring home, let him lug everything around in his backpack for a while as you continue to reinforce his organizational systems. He needs the security of carrying everything he owns while he learns to trust the setup you've created together. When he believes he can rely on himself to bring home just what he needs, he will be able to empty out his backpack.

will serve as a reminder to keep things in order and as a guide when he wants to reorganize his backpack.

- **Music, games, and other electronic equipment** should (ideally) be kept in a separate compartment in the backpack.

- **Extracurricular equipment** may not fit in your child's backpack so you and your child should try to find alternate solutions. RollerBlades, for example, can often be clipped on to the backpack instead of taking up space inside it. Sheet music, on the other hand, can easily fit in the backpack, although you don't want a year's worth building up. Try to help your child find solutions that work, but again, don't let it turn into a battle.

KEEP IT UP

- **Go through the backpack on a regular basis together with your child** until he gets the hang of it. Some students will master the concept in two months and others may need a full school year or even two. The ultimate goal is for your child to acquire the skill and be able to maintain the backpack on his own.

- **Regular maintenance won't take long and it will make a huge difference.** Your child should pick a day of the week to pull out stray papers and candy wrappers and put them where they belong. Sunday is a good day to go through the backpack. Your child can set the tone for the week and feel in control when he gets to school on Monday morning. Younger students in particular like to mimic their parents, preparing side by side for the week ahead. In general, weekends are better than weeknights for this task, but if your child prefers to dismantle his backpack on a Wednesday night that's fine, as long as it gets put back together in time for school.

- **Think of your child's backpack and locker as you think of your own briefcase or pocketbook.** You know when it's disorganized and out of control, when you can't find your keys or planner or lip balm, and it's crammed with old receipts and dusty breath mints. You know when you need to clean it out, and your child knows when his backpack and locker need to be organized. When it's easy to do and your child sees the benefits, the practice will become routine.

A Good Start

Disorganized children, like disorganized adults, can't sustain systems and routines by themselves at first. You have to reassemble, reexamine, and reinforce the systems until your child has internalized them. Becoming better organized will lead to greater success in school and more self-confidence, but it's not a one-stop fix. There will always be good days and bad days, and that's not something that changes as you grow older. There will be days when everything goes wrong and falls apart; the key is *knowing how not to fall apart with it.* It's important for your child to understand that this is a part of life and that if he has a system that works for him and the skills to reassemble it, he'll be able to get back on track right away. He shouldn't beat himself up or throw in the towel when something goes wrong. The goal is to expect things to go wrong at some point and to be confident in the fact that he can handle it.

CHAPTER 4

Traveling Paper: The Binder-Based and Accordion File-Based Systems

Now that you've examined the contents and state of your child's backpack and locker, you should have a sense of how much paper she's dealing with and how she handles it. The next step is to create a traveling paper system that will enable her to find what she needs when she needs it. This is a good step to do early in the organizing process because it allows your child to be creative and requires her to make choices. The more involved she is in the process the better she will be able to create solutions that work for her individual learning style. The goal is to design a system that will be easy to use and easy to maintain. It's not about being neat, and it's not about banishing loose papers from the backpack forever. It's about teaching your child the *process* of creating a paper flow system and helping her discover the *logic* behind it.

This is a tangible exercise with visible results. A paper flow system provides instant gratification: by the end of the

HOW LONG WILL THIS TAKE?

This depends on how fast your child works and how quickly she makes decisions. It should take between one and three hours to set up the complete paper flow system, including the backpack, locker, binder/accordion file, and desktop file box.

session your child has created something she can use the next day in school. The first time she can locate a homework assignment with ease and hand it in on time she will know that her new system works. When she begins to experience success in school as a result of these changes, she will follow you into deeper waters.

Leaving the Comfort Zone: Being Different

Grace, like most seventh graders, used separate spiral notebooks and individual folders for each of her subjects. Unfortunately this system wasn't working for her—there were always loose papers that never made it into folders and notebooks that never made it back to the classroom. When Grace found herself in class without the right notebook, she would just take notes in whatever notebook she pulled out of her bag. This meant that when she came home at night she spent endless hours trying to find her notes and figure out where she wrote her homework down. There were too many elements in her setup to keep track of and the resulting confusion was beginning to affect her grades.

At our first meeting Grace and I decided to transfer her papers over to a binder-based system. Instead of using individual notebooks and folders for each of her five subjects we combined everything in a single three-ring binder. The binder provided space for in-class note taking as well as storage for loose paper, such as handouts, homework assignments, and returned tests. Grace chose the binder she liked and picked the colors, sequence, and setup she wanted to use.

As we assembled the new binder, I was impressed by how patiently Grace worked. Everything was going smoothly until Grace's mom dropped in to see how we were doing. Grace suddenly fell apart. She announced hysterically that she *hated* the binder, and soon she was in the middle of a full-blown meltdown. It became clear, through her tears, that Grace was distraught at the thought of being different from the other kids in her class. I was shocked—she had been so quiet and polite that I had no idea she was so unhappy! Grace's mother, in the meantime, was so upset by her daughter's reaction that she flew off the handle at *me*.

Once I could think straight, I approached Grace and, making sure her mom was listening, talked about the new system we had put together. I asked Grace to try the binder out just for the remainder of the week, and I promised that if it didn't work I would return and put everything back the way I found it. I was shaken by her mom's anger, but I understood what had happened. When Grace turned on her mother in frustration, her mother turned on me. Had I not been there, Grace's mom might have turned the anger right back on her daughter and they would never have settled on a solution for her papers. If this happens while you are working with your child, stay as calm as possible. Try not to react the way you normally might when she's pushing your buttons. Focus on your goal and help your child fix what's not working.

When I called Grace's mother at the end of the week I learned that Grace was thrilled with her binder. It turned out that all of her classmates loved the "cool new system" and wanted to know where they could get one just like it.

At the end of the school year I received a note from Grace's mother.

Dear Donna,

> *Grace is just starting exams and the whole studying process is so much easier because of the system you set up for her. In fact, the whole semester has been organized and smooth. We both thank you!*

> *Have a great summer and we'll see you in September.*

ANALYSIS

■ Being different or sticking out in a classroom is difficult for most adolescents. Try to find a balance between letting your child stay in her comfort zone and encouraging her to try something new.

■ If your child is reluctant to do things differently, ask her to try out the system for a week and see how it goes. Sometimes she may need a gentle (and respectful) push. Check in with her to see if it's working or if it needs to be revised.

■ The more involved your child is in choosing what her system looks like and how it works, the more likely she'll be to use it. Even though Grace initially resisted the new binder, it worked for her because she had made so many of the decisions about how it was designed.

Leaving the Comfort Zone: Being Flexible

The binder system suited Grace because it allowed her to keep all of her notes and handouts for every subject in one place, giving her only one thing to keep track of instead of ten. But binders don't work for everybody. Some students find them uncomfortable to write in, and some school desks are too small to hold an open binder. When I started working with students years ago I put most of them into binders, but lately more students have been choosing other options. When I come across a student who carries a binder back and forth to school every day but shoves all of her notes and loose papers into folders, it's clear the binder is serving no purpose and there's no reason for her to keep it. The accordion file–based system described later in the chapter would suit her needs better. The goal is to remain open-minded as you search for a system that works for your child.

Be flexible. Your child may come up with solutions that aren't ones you would have chosen. Trust her instincts. There are also some kids who will resist any attempt to alter the systems they're comfortable with. Some kids can handle individual notebooks or binders, others can't. Work with your child. If your child refuses to give up her multiple notebooks and folders, focus on what she *can* do to make the system work more effectively. Give in on the notebooks in exchange for her agreeing to clear out loose papers on a regular basis. If multiple folders aren't working, she can put all loose papers into a single folder and clean that out regularly.

The concept of organization so eluded one sixth grader I worked with that for years he refused to change the system we set up during our first session. The system worked for Nick and gave him a sense of control; he didn't want to let go of anything for fear of losing the success he'd found. As he progressed through school I pointed out ways in which his school needs were changing and suggested that he make at least some minor changes to his system. But Nick refused to alter his paper setup in any way—the names of the subjects, the order of the subjects, the color scheme. The system had produced positive results for him and he had become inflexible.

Nick's rigidity was as disconcerting to me as other students' overflowing, out-of-control paper. My work with him was focused more on his inflexibility than on the actual system we set up. It took Nick three years to acknowledge that perhaps the system wasn't working as well as it used to. When he began high school he was finally able to let go of his old binder setup and create a new one that suited his current needs.

Discover Your Inner Sleuth

Some clues about what works and what doesn't work for your child are as obvious as finding class notes in the wrong notebook. Others take a bit more detective work. It's your job to listen for the clues that your child inadvertently offers. Sometimes a seemingly insignificant detail turns out to be the key to understanding what your child needs. I worked with Sam after his first day of sixth-grade classes. Although he'd been in school for fewer than eight hours, there were already pages of notes torn out and floating loosely in his binder. When I asked Sam why he had ripped the pages out, he shrugged and answered, "I don't know."

Sam's school required that he use a three-ring binder divided into five sections, one for each subject. Working within these parameters, we set up a binder in the traditional Organized Student method. When, forty-five minutes into the session, Sam had to write something down, he turned to the proper section of his binder and *tore out a sheet of paper.* I was struck by Sam's decision. His instincts were right—he turned to the correct section of his binder—but then he ripped the page out, making it irrelevant what section it came from! It was a small detail, but it registered. I asked him again, "Why don't you write directly in your binder?"

His answer turned the entire session around. "I don't like writing in the binder. The rings annoy me."

I thought for a moment. "Are you left-handed?"

"Yes."

A-ha.

This single, easy-to-miss detail gave me the insight I needed to create a system that would work for him. We switched from a binder-based system to a separate pad and accordion–file system. The solution for Sam was to take notes all day on a three-hole-punched pad of lined paper instead of in a binder. The pad was much more comfortable to write in than a binder and all of his class notes remained in one place instead of flying around in his backpack. Loose papers, such as handouts, homework, and returned tests, were stored in an accordion file.

His binder was kept at home, basically serving as a filing system for finished work and class notes once a unit was completed.

Sam transferred his class notes from the pad to the appropriate sections in his accordion file once a week under my supervision or under the supervision of his parents, until he got the hang of it. He was able to carry all of the notes and handouts he needed for class without lugging a huge binder around. Whenever a teacher announced an upcoming binder check, Sam would simply bring in the updated loose-leaf binder from home for the teacher to review.

While it wasn't immediately clear to me why Sam was tearing pages out of his binder to take notes, his counterintuitive behavior was a red flag. I kept my eyes open for an explanation, and that explanation turned out to be the key to creating a better paper-flow system for him. Once we made the connection between Sam's being left-handed and his resistance to the binder, we were able to use it to come up with a system that fit the way he worked. We were also able to incorporate the school's requirements into the system in a way that met both Sam's needs and those of his teachers.

ANALYSIS

■ There are reasons why students don't like particular systems, although the reasons are not always clear. Look for the root of the problem and go from there. The smallest detail can be the key to the right solution for your child—keep your eyes and ears open!

■ You can find ways to accommodate teachers' requirements and still create a system that works for your child.

Accommodating Teachers' Requirements

Some teachers request individual binders or notebooks; others want students to subdivide a subject into more specific headings. When your child has a hard time keeping track of *one* notebook or getting her papers home *at all,* it's going to be extremely difficult for her when school requirements get more complicated. Create a system that meets your child's needs first, and then modify it to meet the teachers' requirements as much as possible. It's often helpful to have a conversation with your child's teacher; you will find that many teachers are open to accommodating students' needs.

If your child's school requires separate spiral notebooks for each subject, you can use three-hole-punched notebooks and have your child keep them in the binder. She can write in the notebooks without removing them from the binder and still use subject dividers and poly envelopes for loose papers and homework.

If your child's science teacher wants her subject divided into multiple sections (class notes, handouts, labs, homework, and tests) it may be too detail-oriented for your child. If she can't get her notes into the rings of her binder, she's never going to keep up with multiple sections. When a system becomes too complicated, the disorganized student will usually abandon it. As with all elements of the organizing system, focus on the big picture first: you want to make sure everything at least makes it into the correct subject. If your child can get all of her science papers into the science section, she's doing well, and you should tell her so. If the teacher still requires that the class papers are broken down further, you may have to separate papers into categories on a regular basis with your child. Remember, however, that you are there to teach your child to maintain this finer level of organization, *not* to do the job for her.

Neatness Counts

While your child may not see the value in organizing her papers, you can assure her that teachers do. As I helped Annie, a fifth grader, clean out her old binder, we came across two returned assignments from the same teacher. Each was a set of five questions. The first one had two incorrect answers, but the writing was sloppy, the paper was creased, and the corner was torn off. Angry red letters across the top of the page read, "Do over!" The second paper had *four out of five* answers wrong, but the paper was in pristine condition. The comment across the top read, "Please do over."

The message was loud and clear: the sloppy paper gave the teacher the impression that Annie didn't care about her class, while the neat paper—even with fewer correct answers— gave the teacher the sense that Annie was making an effort. Organizing your child's papers will not only help her find what she needs, but it will also make her efforts clear to others.

WORKING WITH YOUR CHILD'S SCHOOL

How do you successfully advocate for your child when something that the school requires doesn't work for her and you want to make a change in the system? You are going to have to assert your child's right to customize her notebooks and homework planner, and you may face resistance. You should discuss your plans with your child's teacher(s) and possibly the school principal, learning specialist, and/or school psychologist, making it clear that you are all part of a single team, the goal of which is to support your child's academic success.

When you speak to members of your child's school you should aim to convey two important points. First, you want to acknowledge that the school has certain requirements and that you respect the philosophy behind these guidelines. Second, you want to demonstrate that your child learns differently from other students and that the changes you propose will enable her to become more organized and efficient. You can include the teacher in the process, perhaps offering her a choice ("Would you like my child to keep her storage binder at home or in the classroom?"). It is important to emphasize that this is a win-win situation; the system you devise with your child will work better for her and will lead towards greater academic success while still meeting the school's requirements.

Assessment

It's important to help your child discover a system that will be compatible with her learning style, habits, and school requirements. Based on your answers to the Assessment Questions you will assemble either a *Binder-Based System* or an *Accordion File–Based System*.

Plan to create a complete paper flow system with your child in a single sitting. This includes traveling paper (this chapter) and paper at home (the next chapter). Complete the Assessment Questions in both chapters before you begin. The more information you have, the better you'll be able to help your child.

To identify your child's habits and preferences and to pinpoint specific areas that give her trouble

- *Where does your child take class notes?*
    - a. In a single three-ring binder
    - b. In several small three-ring binders
    - c. On paper floating loosely in an otherwise empty binder
    - d. In a large (five-subject) spiral notebook
    - e. In several single-subject spiral notebooks
    - f. What class notes?

- *How are class notes arranged?*
    - a. Notes are separated by subject (English notes are in the English section, math notes are in the math section).
    - b. Individual subjects contain notes from several other classes.
    - c. Notes are neat and organized in all but one subject.

    d. Notes are arranged chronologically, dated at the top of each page.

    e. Notes appear to have no logical order.

    f. Class notes reflect the current unit being studied in school.

    g. Class notes date back to the first day of school.

- *Where are all the loose papers?*
  a. Stored neatly in folders, separated by subject
  b. Hole-punched and placed in the corresponding subjects of a binder
  c. Neatly stored except for the papers in one particular subject
  d. Crammed randomly into folders
  e. Stuck in between pages of a binder or notebook
  f. All over the backpack
  g. All over the house
  h. There are no loose papers.

- *What is the classroom setup? (If your child changes rooms throughout the day, find out the following information about each classroom.)*
  a. Are desks set up individually, or do the students sit and work in groups?
  b. Are desks and chairs separate, or do the desks consist of a surface attached to the arm of a chair?
  c. How large is the surface of the desk? (Large enough to open a binder? Large enough to open a binder *and* a textbook?)

Ask the following assessment questions *for each of your child's subjects* in order to determine what the school requires you to incorporate into your child's system

- *What are the teacher's requirements?*
    a. Students must use separate binders or spiral notebooks for the subject.
    b. The subject must be subdivided within a binder that contains all other subjects (i.e., English subdivided into: class notes, homework, spelling, grammar, literature, and journal).
    c. Students are asked to hand in homework or in-class quizzes on separate sheets of lined paper.
    d. Binders will be checked periodically.
    e. It doesn't matter how your child takes notes or keeps her papers.
    f. Other: _____.

- *Assess the teacher's personality*
    - Obviously you're going to get a somewhat biased answer to this one. What you're really looking for is a sense of how flexible or inflexible the teacher is. Will he ask your child to set up a particular paper system but never look at it again? Or will there be regular binder checks, so you'd better stick to the letter of the law?

Based on your answers to the Assessment Questions, you should be able to determine the type of system that will work best for your child. Below are some specific scenarios you can use as guidelines.

- If your child's notebook or binder is basically in order except for one section that's a mess, you can assume that the problem is not a general one and you will not need to revamp her entire paper flow system. Try to determine why the particular subject is out of order and address the issue accordingly.
  - It's possible that the teacher rushes the students, lets them out of class late, or doesn't give them time to put away their work. In that case, you should spend some time with your child sorting through the loose papers and class notes at home and devise a system together for keeping up with the paper flow from that class.
  - It's also possible that your child is having difficulty with the content of the class, in which case you should address the issue with your child and your child's teacher or any other school officials who might be helpful.
- If your child carries a binder, but there are no papers actually inside the three rings, or if loose papers are shoved haphazardly into folders, a binder system may not be right for her and an accordion file–based system may be the answer.
- If your child has several spiral notebooks, but each is filled with notes from other classes, get everything into one large spiral notebook or a binder.
- If your child finds it uncomfortable to write in a three-ring binder or if there's not enough room to open a binder

on the school desks, set her up with an accordion file and pad instead of a binder.

- If a teacher is strict and has requirements that don't work for your child, you need to speak with the teacher or a guidance counselor.

Stocking Up

Because this is the area of organizing that allows for the most creativity and flexibility, I like to offer students a wide range of supplies to choose from when setting up their paper flow systems. When I meet a student I come equipped like a stationery store. You can also provide your child with enough options to get her involved so that she will enjoy the process and be invested in its outcome.

Based on the assessment questions and a discussion with your child, decide whether a binder-based or accordion file–based system will work best for her. If you're not sure which one to choose, purchase supplies for both systems and return the items she doesn't use. Depending on how interested your child is in picking out the specific supplies, do one of the following:

1. **Bring home multiple options.** Gather a selection of supplies that correspond to the system(s) you've decided upon (see "Gather Supplies" on page 80 and pages 90–92 for specific suggestions). Choose a range of colors and designs whenever possible.

- Most stores will let you return unused supplies within a certain time period. While this means an extra trip to the store, it's worth it if you're able to take the focus off academics, make the process fun, and help your child achieve success.
- Get a sense of your child's style and preferences before you go to the store by showing her pictures of supplies from this book or from an office supply catalog (paper or online).

2. **Bring your child with you to the store.** Do this only after you've answered the Assessment Questions and determined what type of system you're going to create. Again, if you're unsure, you may want to purchase supplies for each.
    - Explain the parameters to your child before you get to the store in order to avoid major arguments and excess spending. ("We're looking for a one-inch binder. Why don't you choose the one you want.")
    - *Really* let her choose what she wants. (Is it more important that she use a particular binder or that she hand her homework in?)

Action: System 1: The Binder

GATHER SUPPLIES
- A 1½-inch binder
- Five- or eight-tab poly subject dividers
- Poly envelopes (one per subject plus two extra)

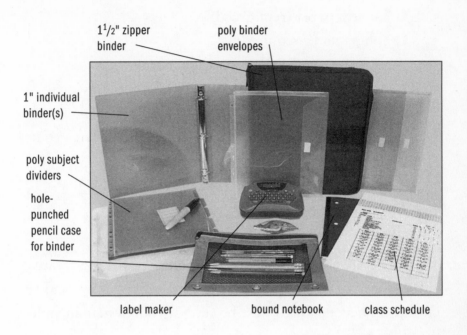

1¹/₂" zipper binder

poly binder envelopes

1" individual binder(s)

poly subject dividers

hole-punched pencil case for binder

label maker   bound notebook   class schedule

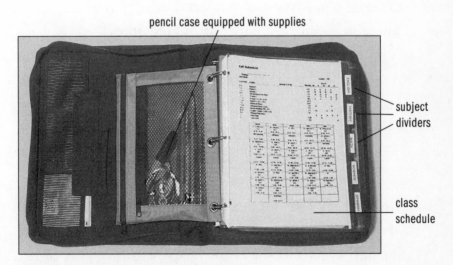

pencil case equipped with supplies

subject dividers

class schedule

The Binder System: supplies and setup.

- Loose-leaf paper (reinforced)
- Graph paper (if required)
- Sheet protector for class schedule
- Three-hole punched bound notebook(s) (if individual notebooks are required)
- Three-hole punched pencil case stocked with items your child needs
- A pen or label maker
- A garbage bag

There are several ways to assemble a binder. Be creative in the materials and colors you use when setting it up, and let your child make choices. Just be certain your system includes the following elements:

- A clearly labeled section in a single large binder *or* an individual binder for each subject
- Three-hole-punched paper for taking notes
- A poly envelope for each subject (to hold loose papers)
- A system for keeping homework visible and accessible

SETTING UP THE BINDER: THE TRADITIONAL WAY
THE BINDER

- **Use a sturdy 1^1/$_2$" binder.** It will be big enough to hold all of your child's papers, no matter how many subjects she has, as long as she keeps the paper flowing. A *zipper binder* is ideal because students can quickly close it and run between classes. If zippering seems like too much of a hassle to your child, use a binder with a Velcro closure so she can at least contain loose papers as she runs from one class to another. She can properly rearrange the loose papers that night when she gets home.

- **Add a pencil case** that fits into the rings of the binder if your child wants one. Fill it with extra pens, pencils, correction fluid, highlighters, and any other supplies your child might need in school.

- **Place a copy of your child's schedule in a sheet protector** at the front of the binder.

INDIVIDUAL SUBJECT SECTIONS

- **Create separate sections in the binder for each subject.** Instead of traditional paper dividers with tabs (which simply separate one section from another), I use poly dividers that slip open or have horizontal pockets. These dividers serve a dual purpose: they separate subjects and also serve as in/out boxes for each class.

THINK ABOUT IT

Papers are often handed to students as the bell is ringing to signal the end of class. Tell your child to just throw the paper into the binder and deal with it later; it's better to quickly store something that can be sorted later than to be late for her next class.

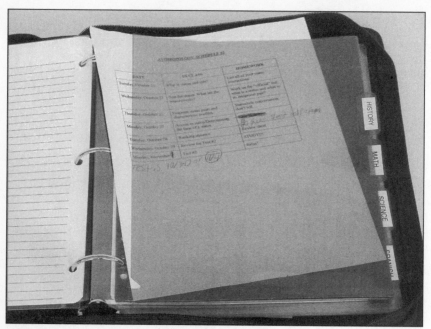

Poly subject divider used as an In/Out box.

- **The In/Out box.** Pocket dividers provide a clear sleeve that can be used to hold homework that needs to be done or that has been completed for each subject or for hand-outs currently being used in class. Every worksheet or reading packet stays with its subject. A student simply has to look through each pocket to see what work still needs to be completed for homework or to find what she needs for class.

- **Another option:** Alternatively, students can keep all of their assignments from each class in one place instead of using the pocket dividers to hold homework. See the section below on "Poly Envelopes."

- **Put lined loose-leaf paper in the binder.** Your child should decide if she wants blank paper in each section or all of the blank paper together in either the front or back of the binder. If your child chooses to have paper in each subject, include extra paper in the back. When she has to turn to the back for paper she'll know it's time to refill her binder.

COLOR AND SEQUENCE

- **Have your child assign each subject its own color.** Students often associate certain colors with specific subjects. I always associate history with the color red because it's such a bloody subject; many students attach their least favorite color to their least favorite subject. There are no

THINK ABOUT IT

Kids are hard on their binders and papers fall out all the time. They hate using adhesive reinforcements and I can't really blame them. To work properly, those sticky little white circles have to be attached to both sides of the page, on all three holes, and most kids don't have the time or patience to bother. Not to mention that if you're disorganized, you usually don't have any reinforcements.

If your kid's really disorganized it's worth it to invest in *reinforced paper*. It costs a bit more than regular paper, but it means your child will probably still have all of her class notes at the end of the semester. You can keep the cost down by getting a group of parents together to buy it in bulk.

wrong answers. It's a way for the student to get involved in the process and make it more meaningful.

- **There are some students for whom color has no meaning.** I once spent a session setting up a student in a color-coded system only to discover that he was color-blind. If you ask your child what color she "sees" a subject in and she has no answer, color probably isn't a key factor for her. In that case, focus on the subject sequence. Your child may want to arrange her subjects alphabetically, in the order her class schedule follows, or in order from most to least favorite. It doesn't matter, as long as it makes sense to her.

- **Use the same color scheme and sequence throughout the rest of the organizing process.** The desktop file box and homework planner should reflect the color and order of subjects used in the binder.

POLY ENVELOPES FOR LOOSE PAPERS

- **Three-hole punched poly envelopes** come in several colors that can be coordinated with the subject dividers. Your child will use these to store loose papers that are traveling back and forth between home and school. This includes homework, returned tests and assignments, worksheets, handouts, reading packets being used in class, and long-term projects.

- **Assign each subject a poly envelope for loose papers.** Depending on how a student uses the subject divider pockets, you can set up the poly envelopes in different ways.

- **Keep all envelopes together in the back of the binder** in the same sequence as the subject dividers.
- **Subdivide the binder sections.** Your child can use the poly envelopes to separate class notes from homework or from tests and quizzes within individual subject sections.

- **Keeping track of homework in one simple step:** If your child prefers to keep all of her assignments in one place (rather than with each individual subject), set up two poly envelopes at the front of the binder, in front of the first individual subject divider. Label them "Homework to Do" and "Homework to Hand In" (or some variation of these titles that your child chooses). When the "Homework to Do" sleeve is empty, your child knows that that portion of her homework is done; when the "Homework to Hand In" sleeve is empty she knows that all of her assignments have been turned in.

> **THINK ABOUT IT**
>
> Some students keep all loose paper in the divider, some keep everything in the back pockets, and some use both. *Set your child up with everything so she has options.* She'll figure out what works for her. The important thing is that she's taken the first step towards paper management.

TO PUNCH OR NOT TO PUNCH?

Most papers teachers give students are not hole-punched, creating an extra step for students to follow in order to stay

> There are three main reasons why I use poly sleeves instead of standard folders:
>
> ■ They're more durable.
>
> ■ They're clear, which means students can see their work. If they can find it they can do it; out of sight is out of mind.
>
> ■ The sleeves can only hold about twenty-five pieces of paper, as opposed to pocket folders, which can hold up to a hundred sheets. A student has to consistently clear out the plastic sleeve in order to maintain her system, whereas a student could continue to fill a standard folder almost indefinitely and never be able to find what she needs.

organized. Many students won't take that step. They don't have a hole punch, or, if there's one in the classroom, the disorganized student doesn't have time to get to it during class. Even for those who have hole punches, things like packets simply won't fit in a standard student's hole punch. The poly envelope allows your child to keep loose paper with the corresponding subject without worrying about an extra step.

Your child will have to take this extra step, however, if her teacher does binder checks. All handouts, assignments, and exams belong in the binder with the current unit, and your child is responsible for getting them there. I recommend that she use poly envelopes to hold loose papers in school, and then punch holes in them and add them to her binder at home.

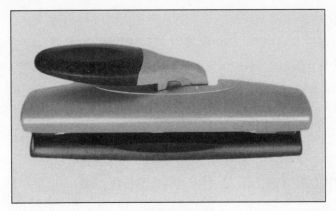

Large-capacity three-hole punch.

Invest in a heavy-duty three-hole punch that can punch up to sixteen pages at a time, and have your child choose a time to add to her binder sections once a week.

OTHER OPTIONS

Some kids simply do not want to use a single binder. If that is the case with your child, let her choose *individual one-inch binders* for each subject or every two subjects and implement the same system as the traditional binder. Use a divider in front of each section and a poly envelope in back of each section to contain homework and loose papers. Choose lightweight poly binders to minimize the weight of your child's backpack.

Other students have schedules or curricula that work well with specific setups. A student whose schedule is consistent throughout the week might want one binder for morning classes and a second binder for afternoon classes. A student in a dual-language school may choose to separate her subjects into binders based on the language in which the subject is taught.

Action: System 2: The Accordion File

Students who aren't interested in using binders at all will use the Accordion File–Based System. This system is suited to kids who find binders uncomfortable, unmanageable, or simply not their style. If the answers to the Assessment Questions indicate that your child prefers to write in a pad or on loose paper, or if she prefers to use individual notebooks for every subject, this is the right system for her. If she tends to lose things, it will be a more challenging system for her to maintain, but if she insists on trying it this way go ahead—you can always make changes later.

Like the binder, this system consists of a place to take notes in class and a place to store loose papers. There are a few options available for note taking and your child should choose the one that makes her comfortable; loose papers will be stored the same way, regardless of her choice.

GATHER SUPPLIES

- A seven- or thirteen-subject accordion file (depending on the number of classes your child is taking). Your best bet is a canvas accordion file with poly dividers that zips closed. Your child can choose from different colors and designs. Just make sure the accordion file is sturdy and fastens shut.

- Paper for taking notes. Your child should choose one of the following:
  - A perforated pad of lined paper (it can be three-hole-punched if your child needs to keep paper in a binder for a binder check or school portfolio)
  - Three-hole-punched loose lined paper
  - Individual bound notebooks, fifty to seventy pages each,

accordion file

note-taking options:
· three-hole punched pad
· spiral notebook
· bound notebook
· composition book

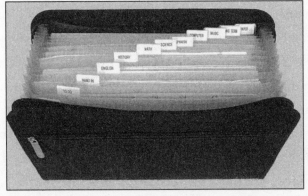

The Accordion File–Based System: supplies and setup.

one for each class (these can be perforated and/or three-hole-punched as well)

- A package of graph paper (if required)
- A class schedule
- A pen or label maker

SETTING UP THE ACCORDION FILE

I've found that this is the most effective way to set up the accordion file. Your child may prefer to keep her homework in the individual subject pockets, but most students find it easier to hold homework for all subjects together up front.

- **Front section** holds your child's homework planner.
- **Label the first pocket** for homework to do ("HW to Do," "To Do").
- **Label the second pocket** for homework to hand in ("HW to Hand In," "Done").
- **Label each additional pocket** with individual subject names.
  - Let your child choose how she wants to label the pockets. If she uses generic subject names instead of specific class names ("math" instead of "algebra") the accordion file can be reused next year without having to be relabeled.
  - Your child can also choose the order of the subjects. They can be arranged alphabetically, according to her schedule, or in any other way that makes sense to her.
- **Tear out a few blank sheets from your child's planner** and keep them in the second-to-last pocket to be used in case she leaves her planner at home.
- **The last pocket** will hold the pad or notebook your child

will use to take notes. Keep some additional loose lined paper in the pocket in case your child leaves her pad at home. If your child needs graph paper keep about twenty sheets in this pocket as well.

- **Be consistent.** Most kids keep their papers *behind* the label for the corresponding subject. If your child wants to keep her papers in front of the labels instead, that's fine; just make sure she's consistent or she'll never be able to find anything.

How to Use the Accordion File-Based System

NOTE TAKING

Your child should be taking notes throughout the day in the manner that is most comfortable and convenient for her. However she chooses to take notes, she should date and list the subject name on every page. This is a habit that takes a while to adopt. Don't nag your child about it, but check in periodically to see if she's doing it or to give her a gentle reminder.

- **Pad of perforated, lined paper.** This is my first choice. It's a single pad of paper, which means your child only needs to keep track of one item, and everything stays in the pad so there are no loose sheets of paper floating around her backpack. At the end of the day or at the end of each week, she will tear out each class's notes and place them in the appropriate section of the accordion file. If she

```
                                                    2/5/06
                                                   Math  HW
  _____
  _____
  _____
```

Sample page labeled with the date, subject, and type of work.

needs to transfer pages into a binder for a binder check she can use a three-hole-punched pad and transfer the papers directly into her binder at home.

- **Individual spiral or bound notebooks.** Some students prefer to keep all of their class notes for each subject in individual notebooks. This eliminates the step of tearing out sheets of paper, but it increases the risk of losing an entire semester's worth of notes. It also means your child is carrying around more paper than she needs. She's not going to be able to store old notes in her file box if she won't tear them out of her notebook. If your child wants to use individual notebooks, however, get the smallest size you can (usually seventy sheets). This will cut down on how much she has to carry, and if she loses a notebook she will have lost only one to three units' worth of notes.

- **Large, multisubject spiral notebook.** Some schools request that children use a single spiral notebook divided into multiple subjects. This is the least desirable option. One section is always finished before the others, and there's no way to add paper to a spiral notebook. If your child carries more than one of these notebooks, she's hauling around several hundred sheets of paper, plus handouts, worksheets, textbooks, and her accordion file. If possible, encourage your child to choose one of the other options.

LOOSE PAPER

- **All loose paper** that pertains to your child's current class unit should be kept in the corresponding section of the accordion file. Once the unit is complete, your child can shift the papers over into her desktop file box, as discussed in the next chapter.
- **Current homework.** Your child has two options:
  1. She can assign the first two pockets of the accordion file (behind the section that holds the planner) to homework for all classes. These are the sections labeled "Homework to Do" and "Homework to Hand In." With this system your child knows that once the first pocket is empty she's completed that part of her homework and once the second pocket is empty she's handed everything in.
  2. She can keep homework to do and completed homework at the front of each individual class section.

Just One More Thing

Although the setup is basic, it's still important to look for signs that your child needs help or further explanation. Alex, an eighth grader, and I decided to transfer his binder-based system into an accordion file–based system. He was happy to make the trade since the binder was too much trouble for him to keep up and now he would have just one pad of paper for taking notes. As I was getting ready to leave, Alex asked me if I could just help him out with one more thing. I said sure, and he handed me the pad of paper.

"Can you tear out the notes for me?" he asked.

I know teenagers can be lazy, but this seemed a little excessive. Wondering if I had heard correctly, I asked, "What do you mean?"

"I can't tear the paper out of the pad." Alex proceeded to show me that he *literally* couldn't tear the paper out of the pad. He was unable to grasp the paper with his fingers, which made it impossible for him to remove the pages.

"Alex, we just set up an entire system based on using this pad to take notes! How can it possibly work if you can't pull the paper out at the end of the day?"

It never occurred to me that this would be a problem. Alex was a tremendous athlete; he played soccer and football and a host of other sports. He had trouble, however, with fine-motor skills. Not knowing that, I could have easily walked out the door, leaving him with a system that he would never be able to use.

"Watch me," I said. I pressed down on the top of the pad with my left hand and slowly pulled the top sheet out with my right. I explained that the pressure helped me tear the paper out evenly and that if I pulled the paper out at an angle it wouldn't rip. Alex tried it himself and was thrilled to find that he could tear the page out.

I never would have known Alex did not possess such a "basic" skill if he hadn't asked me to help him. When I went back to see him a few weeks later, his desk was clear of all the loose sheets of paper he used to use for taking notes and jotting down ideas. Instead there were two pads of paper full of writing, several pages of which he proudly ripped out for me.

Continuing the Paper Flow

Whichever system your child chooses, the important thing is that she maintain it. The next step, the desktop file box, helps ensure that your child's traveling paper system doesn't grind to a halt halfway through the semester. Create the binder and desktop file box together so the paper flow system can get off the ground all at once.

CHAPTER 5

Where Paper Lives at Home: The Desktop Filing System

The disorganized student lives in fear of being caught without the one thing he needs. He's terrified of being called on to read from a handout he doesn't have or being asked to refer back to an old assignment he left at home. His solution is to carry *everything*—every handout, every worksheet, every test he's ever gotten back—in his backpack, to and from school, every day.

There are two main problems with this approach. The first is that the student's backpack ends up weighing more than the student himself. The second is that carrying everything in a disorganized fashion doesn't allow him to access *anything* quickly enough to be of any use. To address these problems, you first need to organize your child's binder and backpack so that there will be an appropriate place for all of the papers he actually needs. When he knows he can quickly find what he's looking for, it will be easier for him to trust himself and let go of the extra paper. Then you need to create an equally logical storage system for paper at home so that your child can regularly shift notes and worksheets out of his binder, notebooks, or accordion file without being afraid that he will never find them again. This brings us to the *Desktop Filing System.*

The file box used in the Desktop Filing System is the first step toward organization at home. It not only lightens the load a student carries on his back but also keeps papers organized for future reference. Using it will teach your child how to re-access information and reduce the panic surrounding midterms and finals by allowing him to easily locate all of the notes, worksheets, tests, and quizzes he needs in order to study. This chapter will take you through the process of setting up and maintaining a Desktop Filing System and creating a place for papers to live in your home.

A Home for Everything

Remember Jack, the high school junior who carried every paper he'd received since the beginning of the year? We spent three hours on the floor separating his notes and papers by subject and rearranging them chronologically. The reason we even bothered with the second step was because Jack had labeled every paper he received with three pieces of information: the date, the subject, and either a "CW," for class work, or an "HW," for homework. Even a student who is completely disorganized physically can have one strong system that keeps him going. If Jack's papers hadn't been labeled it would have taken several *additional* hours to decipher everything. It wouldn't have been worth it; we would have simply put his current papers in order and filed the rest by subject.

The next step was to decide what went back in Jack's binder and what was going to stay home. In order to do this we had to figure out what he was currently learning in each class to see what he needed to have on hand. We started with Ancient History. Jack's class notes, tests, and reports broke down chronologically to cover Mesopotamia, Ancient Egypt, and Ancient Greece. Greece was the unit he was currently studying, so we separated everything relating to Greece and filed the rest in his desktop file box. All of the current class notes, homework, and quizzes were stored in his binder and Jack no longer had to lug around hundreds of unnecessary sheets of paper on a daily basis.

It was clear that Jack's ability to do work was not the issue; he was very bright, he took notes in class, and he did his homework. The problem was that he could never find what he needed, whether it was homework to hand in or class notes to study from. It took two people *three hours* to sort through everything in Jack's backpack. How quickly could he possibly have found anything on his own? When the time came to prepare for exams it was easier for him to go back to the textbook and start from scratch than to wade through a mountain of paper searching for relevant material. This meant Jack spent more time doing work he'd already done and less time studying.

ANALYSIS

■ A student needs to be able to find what he needs quickly; carrying around every paper he owns is going to make his life harder instead of easier.

■ Encourage your child to get in the habit of dating his papers. It will save time and energy when he wants to reconstruct his class notes and homework in the future.

■ As midterms and finals approach, many students spend a lot of time organizing instead of studying. The desktop file box allows a student to access his materials quickly and easily instead of wasting time hunting and gathering.

Assessment

The answers to these Assessment Questions will help you create a logical system and place for your child's desktop file box. Combine these questions with the assessment questions from the last chapter so that you can complete the paper flow system all at once.

To help determine where to keep the file box

- *Where does your child do his homework?*
    a. At a desk in his room
    b. On the floor in his room
    c. Anywhere *but* in his room

    d. All over the house

    e. At a specific spot outside of his room (at a desk or at the kitchen table)

    f. At school

    g. In different locations because he splits the week between two homes

- *Where are your child's papers?*
  a. Stacked neatly in piles on his desk
  b. Covering the desk, under the bed, and shoved into drawers
  c. All over the house
  d. All in his backpack
  e. What papers?

- *Is there a paper trail wherever your child goes?*

- *Does your child have a desk that can accommodate the desktop file box, either in his room or wherever else in the house he does his homework?*
  - If not, think about a place where the file box can live that will be user-friendly (on a nearby shelf or windowsill, or near a computer table where he works). The box should ideally rest on a raised surface instead of on the floor.
  - Out of sight is out of mind. Think like a child—when your child wants something from you he's relentless. If you want your child to use the file box, keep it right in front of him.

THINK ABOUT IT

Many desks come with built-in file drawers, but most kids do not use file drawers successfully. The disorganized child isn't going to take the extra step to open the drawer or even to lift the lid of a closed file box. It's one step too many, and once papers disappear into a closed drawer or box he'll forget about them.

To determine how you will set up the desktop file box

- *Does your child's school use a portfolio system?*
  - In a portfolio system a teacher holds on to students' schoolwork throughout the year in order to document and track their progress. If this is the case in your child's school, you probably won't find much paper floating around. Some teachers, however, collect only sample work from a student, such as the papers and exams of which the student is proudest. A disorganized student often can't find those papers when he needs to. A file system at home will help organize the papers so they can be found and turned in when the teacher asks for them.

- *List the subjects that your child is studying in school.*

- *List the extracurricular interests and social events that your child needs to keep track of:*
  - Team practices and games
  - Club meeting dates and projects
  - Parties

- Community service
- Religious school

- *Assess your child's organizational capabilities.*
  - Would you be happy if your child could just get everything from one subject into the appropriate file?
  - Does you child have the ability and temperament (i.e., patience) to break the system down further? If yes, would he do this by:
    - Filing papers by subject in chronological order?
    - Clipping together completed units within each subject?
    - Separating class notes, homework, tests, and quizzes within each unit in order to study for unit tests, midterms, and finals?

HOW LONG WILL THIS TAKE?

The desktop file box will probably take twenty to forty-five minutes to set up. It should be completed in your first session, together with the other elements of the paper flow system.

Action: Set Up the Desktop Filing System

Unlike the traveling paper system, the desktop filing system does not allow for much flexibility. Still, you want to set up the desktop file box with your child to ensure that he will be invested in its success.

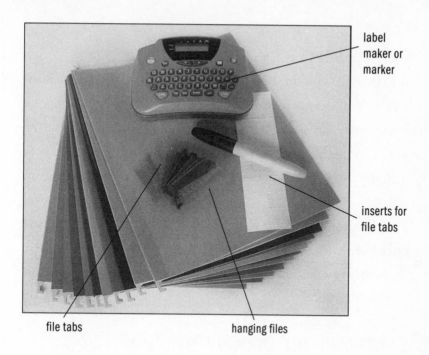

label maker or marker

inserts for file tabs

file tabs

hanging files

The Desktop File Box: supplies and setup.

GATHER SUPPLIES

- **A (10-inch) sturdy plastic desktop file box,** open (without a lid). You do not want to use a crate. Although it may be inexpensive and easy to find, it will never fit on a desk; the desktop file box may be harder to find, but it works.
- **Ten to twelve hanging file folders,** ideally in different colors.
- **Plastic tabs and blank inserts** to label the files. (These come with the hanging files.)
- **A monthly calendar** ($8\frac{1}{2}$" x 11") to hang over the front of the file box.

SETTING UP THE DESKTOP FILE BOX

- **Decide on an order for the files.** Ideally you want to follow the sequence already established in the binder or accordion file. Some students will, however, find it important to create a different order for the file box. As long as it makes sense to your child, go ahead. It can always be changed later.
- **Label the files.** Those little tabs are there for a reason! Clearly label each file. If your child's handwriting is illegible, consider printing the labels out on a computer or using a label maker. It's important that the files appear uniform, neat, and attractive. And it's a good opportunity to get your child involved by choosing the font style or by using the label maker.
- **Use generic subject headings.** Instead of "algebra" label the file "math." Your child will then be able to use

the same file for the next four to six years without rela-
beling it.

- **Place the tabs on the front of the file, not the back.** This
  way the name of the file won't be obstructed by the papers inside. It also keeps the tab from coming out when
  the file is pulled open.
- **Make the file box the epicenter of your child's activities.** It
  should be used to organize multiple aspects of a student's
  life, not just academics.

PERSONAL FILES

The file box does more than help your child organize his
schoolwork; it encourages him to take responsibility for
tracking different elements of his life. The Assessment Questions will help determine which extracurricular files might be
relevant to your child. When you add them to the file box,
keep them separate from the class files. School subjects come
first and behind them are the personal files. Following are
some examples of some personal files students have used:

- **Instructions** (instructions and manuals for games, elec-
  tronic equipment, etc.)
- **Art** (drawings, doodles, and small artwork)
- **Writing or ideas** (creative writing and ideas)
- **Music** (sheet music or song lyrics)
- **Clubs** or a specific club, such as Newspaper (school club
  and committee schedules and information)
- **Team** or a specific team, such as Basketball (team sched-
  ules and phone numbers)

- **Summer** (summer camp and program information and newsletters)
- **Religious school** (religious school notes and information)
- **Phone numbers** (copies of class lists as well as miscellaneous scraps of paper with phone numbers scribbled on them)
- **Invitations**

WHAT *NOT* TO KEEP IN THE FILE BOX

- Magazines
- Large projects
- Anything bulky that takes up too much space

The Rules of Filing

In any well-functioning office you will find an extensive filing system. You know it's a good system if the person in charge of the files is absent and everyone can still find exactly what he or she needs; papers can be easily accessed and work can continue to flow. If they're *your* files, this means you can go on vacation without being hunted down by a coworker searching for the year-end report. The desktop file box is your child's introduction to the understanding and practice of a good filing system. It should serve him well in school and far into the future, but it needs to be taught in increments, at a pace he can keep up with.

You want your child to meet with success every step of the way. Positive feedback and results will encourage him to stick with the system; start with general filing concepts and not with details. Then, depending on your child's ability to put theory into practice, you can advance to more specific filing rules. If, for example, your child is like Grace, whose papers were always in the wrong subjects' notebooks, don't bother discussing how to file papers chronologically. Focus on getting your child to put all of the math papers into the math file and the history papers into the history file. When the ability to file in general categories becomes automatic, you can break the process down further.

After your child masters filing by subject, you can teach him to file chronologically. This is where dating papers really comes in handy. Papers can be filed chronologically in two ways: back to front or front to back. Businesses traditionally file papers back to front, with the most recent invoice, medical record, or revised contract up front. While this makes sense in most business contexts it is generally not ideal for students. Your child is going to have to study from the filed papers and he is going to be expected to review notes, handouts, and quizzes from the beginning of a unit or semester. The best way to study is to review the course as it was taught, and the easiest way to do that is to keep papers in the order in which they were written or received.

Most subjects are taught in a specific order for a reason;

one event or skill refers to or builds on the previous one. Your child will need to follow the logic of the material in order to comprehend what he is studying, and he can do this easily if the notes follow the sequence of the class. In addition, class notes and worksheets are often double-sided (written on both the back and front), so arranging pages in the order in which they were written makes them much easier to follow. While I recommend this method of filing, I'm not too concerned with how students file as long as they're consistent.

Your child may reach a point where he is able to take the system one step further by clipping each completed unit together. This step takes a little extra time and, while not pivotal, does make things easier when he is studying for midterms and finals. He may also want to separate class notes from homework, quizzes, and tests within an individual unit. Some teachers require students to do this, although I don't think it's always helpful, since your child should be studying *all* relevant materials in the order in which they were taught. However, if your child has mastered the art of filing and deems this helpful, let him go ahead. The more involved he is in the process the better. Most students need to start with the basic system and meet with success there. Over the next year(s) you may be able to implement some of the more advanced steps. For additional tips on filing you can refer to the Esselte-Pendaflex® Web site (www.pendaflex.com), click on "Free Templates," and download "The Pendaflex® How to File Guide."

How Often Should Your Child File?

Ideally, your child should file frequently enough to keep his paper flowing. The desktop file box is meant to store papers he doesn't need in school. If your child's backpack or binder is overflowing again, it's clearly time to file. If your child is able to keep the paper moving, it will take less time for him to keep everything in order.

The more frequently your child files the less time it will take overall. Do not, however, expect him to do it every night. Think of this the way you think of your handbag or briefcase. You don't need to go through it nightly, but if you clean it out regularly you can restock the essentials and unload the things you don't need to be carrying around so you can find what you need when you need it.

> ## FREQUENT FILING
>
> If your child files once a week it should take about five minutes to get the whole job done. If he files once every two weeks, it will take about fifteen minutes, and if he does the job only once a month it will end up taking about forty-five minutes.

Encourage your child to shoot for every one to two weeks when it comes to filing. Sunday night is a good time to do it, or whatever time is designated for homework on the weekend. As with organizing his backpack, this allows your child to get into the habit of starting out the school week organized. You can, however, be flexible. Let your child choose a day for filing that works best for him, as long as it remains as consistent as possible. For the first several months your child should actually schedule the filing time in his homework planner. It takes twenty-one consecutive days to start a habit; filing should become a regular part of your child's routine.

Sometimes a student has so much paper by the end of his first semester that he needs to empty out his file box. If this is the case with your child, or if he simply wants to clean house and start fresh in the new semester, have him remove each subject from the file box, one at a time. He should clip each stack of papers together and label the first page with a sticky note that indicates the subject, his grade, and the semester ("History, 7th grade, 1st semester"). He should then gather all of the piles and store them in a poly envelope and label the envelope ("7th grade—1st semester"). The envelope should be stored someplace accessible, like in a desk drawer or on a nearby shelf, in case he needs to return to the notes to study.

Just in Case

The desktop filing system is designed to help students like Jack, who can't find anything even though they have it all, as well as students like Alana, who have everything but lose it all. Alana's mom called me in February at her wits' end. Her sixth grader had been having trouble all semester. She was turning her assignments in late or losing them, forgetting to bring home the books she needed for homework, and misplacing her belongings all the time. Every day there was some nonacademic issue involving Alana's forgetfulness or disorganization that interfered with her success in school. Alana tried hard and did her work, but the stress caused by her inability to keep track of things led to tension in the family every night.

The straw that broke the camel's back came on December 23, when Alana returned home freezing because she had *lost her coat*. Alana's mom was distraught—not only did she have to buy her daughter another coat, but her child had been wandering around in twenty-degree weather wearing only a sweater! Alana's mom told her that she knew it was hard for Alana to keep track of things and she didn't really know how to help anymore, but there was a lady who helped kids get organized. Alana was relieved.

Alana was wonderful to work with and she made a lot of progress in a short time. She was like a sponge. There wasn't a thing she didn't understand and implement. I met with her on a regular basis (first every two weeks, then every three weeks) and monitored her improvement. We set up systems that helped her keep track of everything, including a desktop file box. By the end of March she had taken a 180-degree turn. Her friends now considered her the most organized kid in the class! When they were assigned a group project, they decided to put Alana in charge of tracking and holding on to everything since she was the most organized.

Alana and her friends worked very hard assembling their project, and Alana kept track of everything in her binder. Then, sometime near the end of April, I got a desperate phone call. Alana was in tears. The report was due in a week, and she had lost her entire binder. I quickly rearranged my schedule so that I could meet with her right away. The good news, although this was not the time to point it out, was that Alana didn't lose an entire year's worth of work since she had already filed a lot of it at home. The bad news was that Alana's habit of losing things now affected more than just herself—she was accountable to her friends, and she was miserable about it.

I helped Alana assemble a new binder so she could move forward with her class work, and her mother supported her through the rest of the process. She assured Alana that she would survive this crisis. She sat with Alana while she cried for three hours and then was forceful about Alana calling everyone to own up to what she did. She remained beside her while Alana made the phone calls and then helped her reconstruct the project. When the dust had settled, I addressed the fact that there would always be good days and bad days. There would be times when Alana was on top of everything and times when something got lost. The smartest thing she could do was be prepared.

Having systems that could be easily reassembled and systems for archiving old work was one important step. A second step focused specifically on long-term projects. We decided that for every research project Alana would make photocopies of the work as she went along. We discussed the fact that people often back up computer data, and it seemed logical to perform the same function with anything else of value that might get lost. Today most people have access to technology, such as copy machines, computers, and scanners, that makes it easy to keep duplicates of important material. This extra step takes time, but not nearly as much time as having to rewrite an entire research paper by yourself.

ANALYSIS

■ For many kids, difficulty with organizational issues is not strictly academic. It flows into all different areas, such as losing money and keys or having a messy bedroom, and it creates tension in their lives and with their families.

■ You don't go from disorganized to perfect in one step—there will be setbacks along the way. Expect them.

■ Establishing a backup system can save hours of work and agony in the future.

■ The attitude a parent takes is pivotal to a child's ability to handle unexpected situations.

Electronic Trends

Some schools are in the process of converting to electronic-based learning. Students take notes on laptop computers, and teachers e-mail lecture outlines to students and post assignments online. In spite of these changes kids are still swamped with paper. Many teachers still use handouts and worksheets; some subjects, like math, require paper-based work; tests are often written on paper; and hard copies of assignments are usually returned with teachers' comments. Kids need some way to store all of the paper they receive. An accordion file can be used to hold loose papers that are being used in class and to transport paper back and forth to school. The desktop file box holds old handouts and returned assignments, and when it's time to study for a test your child can print out all of his class notes and keep them in the file box.

Whether or not your child's school is "going electronic," your child probably does some work on a computer. It's just as important for your child to organize his electronic work, whether you have a computer at home or he transports his work on disks or CDs. The guidelines for organizing electronic work are basically the same as they are for paper: everything should be grouped by subject and clearly and consistently labeled. Following are some specific suggestions for organizing your child's documents and files.

If you have a computer at home:

- *Create a folder on the desktop labeled with your child's name and grade or the school year (for example, "Jake— Grade 7" or "Jake—2005–06").*

- *Within this folder create individual folders for each of his subjects labeled with the subject name and your*

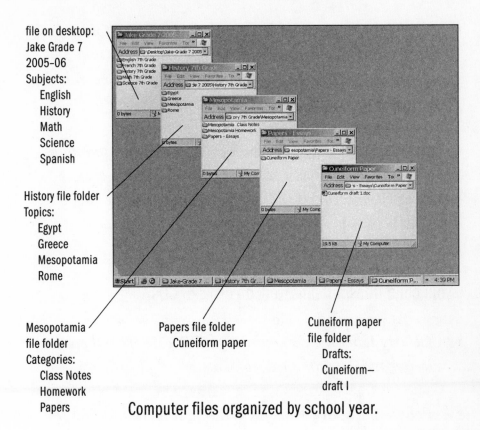

file on desktop:
Jake Grade 7
2005-06
Subjects:
  English
  History
  Math
  Science
  Spanish

History file folder
Topics:
  Egypt
  Greece
  Mesopotamia
  Rome

Mesopotamia
file folder
Categories:
  Class Notes
  Homework
  Papers

Papers file folder
  Cuneiform paper

Cuneiform paper
file folder
Drafts:
  Cuneiform—
  draft I

Computer files organized by school year.

child's grade or the school year ("History—Grade 7" or "History—2005–06").

- *Within each subject folder create additional folders for each individual unit.*

- *Within each unit folder create three separate folders: Class Notes, Homework, Long-term Assignments. All class notes or homework assignments pertaining to a specific unit can be filed together ("Class Notes—Unit 1—Mesopotamia").*

- *Within Long-term Assignments create a new folder for every assignment* so that all drafts pertaining to a particular paper or project can be found in one folder (*"Paper—Cuneiform: The First Writing System"*).

- *Create a logical system for numbering drafts and notes in the title of each document.* (*"Cuneiform—draft 1," "Cuneiform—draft 2," "Class Notes—week 3,"* or *"Class Notes—9.10–9.15"*)

If your child transports his work on disks or CDs

- *Clearly label the disk holder or CD case* with the subject(s) and dates of the documents.

- *Follow the above steps for creating folders and files* for individual subjects and assignments.

Conquering the Chaos

The amount of paper passing through students' hands has grown exponentially over the past decade and a half. When I started organizing students I used a filing box that was six inches deep and it got a student through the entire school year. Today the box I use has almost doubled in size and I often have to empty it after the first semester. There are times when I know I could use an even bigger box, but it wouldn't fit on top of a desk. As the mountains of paper grow, your child's skill at organizing, storing, and re-accessing paper needs to grow too. A user-friendly filing system and regular maintenance on a set schedule will help your child conquer the chaos.

CHAPTER 6

Settling Down to Work: The Desk and the Portable Office

The desk serves as both a workstation and as the center of a student's life. If you think of your child's room as a microcosm of your home, you'll understand that she needs enough storage space to hold and display everything she owns. While adults have entire homes to exhibit collections of books, stereo equipment, and memorabilia, kids have only their rooms. Fads come and go quickly (remember Smurfs? Pogs? Beeping animal keychains?) and collections are replaced often. Where do old collections go to die? Straight into desk drawers. Often kids are not taught to store or throw away things they no longer want. Old collections overtake the little storage space they have and leave no room for the things they actually need. By teaching a student how to sort, purge, and organize, you can help her make her space more efficient. She will be able to locate what she needs, whether it's school supplies or computer games. Plus, she will be able to put everything back in its place so that she can find it again the next time she wants it.

Anthony was the seventh grader who never worked at his desk, mostly because it was filled with baseball cards instead of school supplies. While not all students work most efficiently at their desks, I thought Anthony should at least have the option of working at his if he wanted to. In order to make the space usable, we cleared the magazines, CDs, and video games off the surface of the desk and set up his desktop file box. We emptied the drawers, dumping the baseball cards into a garbage bag to deal with later and tossing the old papers. We outfitted the desk with school supplies and used the remaining drawers to house some of his collections; whatever did not belong in the desk went to live somewhere else.

By clearing away most of the visual clutter on and around Anthony's desk we were able to create a space that was conducive to studying rather than distracting. We added a bulletin board behind the desk that became the central location for things Anthony needed to get to quickly. We stuck his bus pass, watch, and basketball schedule onto the bulletin board, along with a large monthly calendar. The calendar would help Anthony keep track of deadlines and vacation days and the bulletin board would help him keep track of everything else. We also cleared off the bookshelf just above his desk and turned it into a home for books he was currently reading, textbooks he was using that year, and a dictionary and thesaurus.

We did not finish the job in one day; I did not expect to. I also did not expect Anthony to suddenly change his habits and start working at his desk. Over time, however, Anthony discovered that the supplies he needed were in his desk drawers and he began to gravitate toward the redesigned workspace.

And as he started to use his desk more regularly, new piles started to form. Anthony and I went back to square one and sorted through the stacks of baseball cards and other items that had migrated back to his desk. This time instead of taking six hours it took fifteen minutes.

Anthony and I met monthly and spent the first fifteen minutes of each session clearing up his desk. Eventually he internalized the process and recognized the value of spending a few minutes every month putting his workspace back in order. Most students, like most adults, do not sort through their desks daily. But making this task a regular part of one's schedule, whether it's weekly, biweekly, or monthly, makes both studying and working more efficient and pleasant. Make sure everything your child uses and needs has a logical place so that it's easy to put things away, and review the process regularly with him until it becomes a part of his routine.

ANALYSIS

■ Kids don't work at desks that are not user-friendly.

■ Organizing papers that travel back and forth to school is the first priority; the desk comes later.

■ Organizing a desk takes time; the project will probably not be completed in a single sitting, so plan accordingly.

■ Don't expect your child to start using his redesigned desk immediately.

■ Stay focused on the task at hand (cleaning out the desk) and not on distractions that come up along the way.

Assessment

Many students do their homework in their rooms but not at their desks, and many more do their homework somewhere else in the home altogether. Some students, like Anthony, have a great desk area that's not set up properly, while others have no desk at all. Some prefer to work near other people, whether that means at the kitchen table or on the living room floor. Many homes have a single, central computer located outside of a student's room.

Additional factors that influence where students work include:

- *Sleeping arrangements. Does your child:*
  - Share a room and a desk?
  - Share a room with a younger sibling who has an earlier bedtime, limiting the amount of time her desk is available?
  - Lack a desk or room for a desk in the room where she sleeps?

- *Specific demands of the homework:*
  - Some projects require more space than a desk can provide.
  - Your child might need help with homework and have to be near someone who can answer questions.

- *Household setup:*
  - A central computer is located outside of the bedroom.
  - Family members work together in a common area.

All of these arrangements mean that a student's books and supplies are often someplace other *than where she is doing her homework.*

The following Assessment Questions focus on your child's room and work habits. Depending on your answers, you or your child will set up a desk and/or a portable office.

To help determine whether a desk or a portable office will better suit your child's needs

- *Where does your child work?*
  - a. At a desk in her room
  - b. On the bed or floor of her room
  - c. In various places throughout the house
  - d. At the kitchen table
  - e. Next to someone else
  - f. In front of the TV
  - g. At school
  - h. Other: _____

- *What equipment is available for your child to use?*
  - a. A desk (is it a regular sized desk or a junior desk?)
  - b. A computer (does it sit on the desk? Is it a desktop or a

laptop? Is the keyboard on the desk or under it? Where in your home is it located?)

c. A printer, scanner, etc. (does it sit on the desk?)

d. File drawers

e. Multiple desk drawers or drawer unit

f. Proper lighting

g. A proper desk chair

h. Other: _____

• *What are your child's living arrangements?*

a. She has her own bedroom.

b. She shares a bedroom with sibling(s).

c. She shares a bedroom with other family member(s).

d. She splits time between more than one home (e.g., divorced family, weekend home).

e. Other: _____

• *What is the ideal study environment for your child?*

a. She needs silence.

b. She works best with music.

c. She needs to work alone.

d. She needs company.

e. She is easily distracted.

f. She gets work done efficiently, regardless of clutter.

g. She needs to lay out everything in order to see what needs to be done.

h. Other: _____

To help determine what type of storage space your child needs

- *What does your child's desk look like?*
  a. It's neat and orderly, with plenty of visible surface area.
  b. Every square inch is covered with piles.
  c. Most of the desk's surface area is taken up by a computer monitor and keyboard.
  d. Drawers are filled with everything but school supplies.
  e. There are no drawers.
  f. There is no desk.
  g. Other: _____

- *What kinds of collections does your child have?*
  a. Baseball cards
  b. Computer games
  c. Jewelry
  d. Makeup
  e. Music
  f. Photographs
  g. Computer equipment
  h. Other: _____

- *Where do the collections live?*
  a. In a desk drawer
  b. On top of the desk
  c. On the floor
  d. Under the bed
  e. In boxes
  f. In the closet

g. Everywhere you look

h. Other: _____

Based on your answers, you will proceed in one of three ways: set up a desk, set up a portable office, or set up both. You will also create proper storage for your child's collections once you see what she wants to keep and how frequently she wants to access her different collections. Use the guidelines below to determine your plan.

- **If your child seems like she would be inclined to use a desk if it were properly arranged,** proceed to "Creating the Ideal Desk." This is likely the case if your child already does most of her work in her bedroom, even if she does it on the floor or on her bed.

- **If you've discovered that your child works all over the house** and will likely continue to do so, create a portable office. Read "Creating the Ideal Desk" first; it contains important information about working with your child, determining her needs, and creating proper storage.

- **If your child does some work at her desk or in her room and some work elsewhere** (because she needs help, shares a room with a sibling who has an earlier bedtime, or simply likes company while she does homework), aim to create *both* a usable desk and a portable office.

Creating the Ideal Desk

In general, a student will work best at a desk in her own room. Having a central location for papers will streamline the homework process and help your child keep track of extracurricular activities. When she can find everything she needs quickly she will be able to start her homework right away.

The ideal desk has two main components: plenty of storage space and plenty of surface area. When I was a kid I had a desk with five drawers on each side. I didn't realize how well designed that desk was until I grew up and started working with students. The most common desks on the market today are outfitted with one or two shallow drawers and a file drawer, none of which are sufficient to meet the needs of today's students. The best option is an L-shaped desk with at least two sets of drawers. It doesn't have to be new or expensive—it can be three sets of plastic drawers and two slabs of Formica. In fact, since it's rather difficult to find the ideal desk today, you may do better assembling one yourself. The L-shaped desk became important for kids as soon as we started plunking computers onto their desks, eliminating most of the workspace.

If you do not have an L-shaped desk, or room for it, any surface will suffice as long as it has enough storage space to hold your child's supplies and enough surface area to allow her to spread out. One side of the desk can be used as workspace and the other can hold a computer (either a monitor with a pullout drawer for the keyboard or a laptop), a second set of textbooks, or reference books your child uses on a regular basis. If your child has a computer on her desk she should be able to shift easily back and forth between work stations, spreading out papers and reference books on one side while writing on the other. There should also be enough surface space to keep the desktop file box and often-used supplies within arm's reach.

The configuration of the desk should be adapted to the individual. Take into account, for example, your child's dominant side (left or right), potential distractions (like windows), and her need for light or sound. If possible, choose an adjustable chair. It will grow as your child does, it's the best bet for children who share a desk, and it's the easiest way to accommodate the different workspace needs of a student. An adjustable chair can be raised and lowered to suit the side of the desk at which your child is working and the type of work she's doing. If your child uses a laptop computer, for example, the height of the desk chair should be adjusted so that her wrists are not angled upwards when she types; keyboard drawers, on the other hand, are better suited to lower chairs. While ergonomics are important, remember that most students aren't spending eight hours a day in front of a computer; you needn't worry too much about the problems that plague so many office workers today.

THE TEENAGER'S TOY CHEST

File drawers are wasted space in a kid's room. These deep drawers often turn into teenager's toy chests. Like their playroom counterparts, they are quickly filled with random objects instead of serving as useful storage. A kid has to dig through stacks of paper and abandoned collections in order to find the one thing she's looking for. Reports disappear into file drawers and emerge years past their deadlines. To a teenager, out of sight is out of mind. Storing papers properly is an important part of the organizing process that leads to academic success, and the desktop file box is a much more visible, accessible, and practical way for teenagers to manage their papers.

If a file cabinet or drawer is already part of the setup you own, there are ways to make efficient use of the space. The key is to use it to house seldom-used items rather than files and papers a student needs to access often. Label some hanging files to store the previous semester's work, completed projects, or computer and game manuals. Alternatively, you can use the file drawer to store extra school supplies. Remove the metal rods used to support hanging files (if you can) and *vertically* arrange items such as three-ring binders, spiral notebooks, and packages of paper in

HOW LONG WILL THIS TAKE?

It depends on how much stuff your child has on and in her desk. I suggest that you set aside an hour and a half for the desk. If you need more time, schedule another appointment with your child.

the drawer. By placing them vertically your child can see what she has and access it quickly, rather than rummaging through piles hoping to find what she needs.

A file drawer holding supplies arranged vertically.

Action: Setting Up the Desk

DIVIDE AND CONQUER

You can avoid being overwhelmed by this project by looking for the smaller, doable tasks that make up the big picture. Do not empty the contents of the desk onto the floor all at once. Instead, start with the desktop. It may take you the full hour and a half just to clear the desktop. If that's the case, congratulate yourselves and clean up. After the surface of the desk is clear, organize the desk one drawer at a time. If you get to a drawer, great! If you get to two drawers, great! If you organize the entire desk in record time, great! Pace yourselves and keep the big picture in mind.

- **Measure** your child's current desk and each of its drawers.
- **Purchase desk accessories and supplies.** Your list should include a pen cup and a desk tray to sort supplies within drawers, as well as any supplies your child doesn't already have at home, such as a stapler and staples, pens and pencils, highlighters, erasers, paper clips, a three-hole punch, printer ink and paper. If your child wants to be included in the decorative decision making, great. Otherwise, pick up the desk accessories yourself. Don't invest too much in them. You can get a perfectly suitable plastic desk tray for $1.99 and you won't be upset when your kid spills Wite-Out all over it.
- **Come armed** with garbage bags, small plastic zipper bags, a handheld vacuum, paper towels, a damp cloth, and spray cleaner. Gather a couple of containers to use as you sort the contents of your child's desk. You can use plastic bins or shopping bags to hold the contents of the desk temporarily and then decide what you will need for long-term storage after the desk has been rearranged.
- **Do a sweep of the desktop,** grouping similar items as you go along (put all loose change in a bag, all magazines in a pile, all papers in a stack). You can use the floor, bed, or any other clear surface as your workspace. Any item you come across that doesn't have an obvious or estab-

lished home should get tossed into a single box or shopping bag.

- **Empty the drawers one at a time,** continuing to use broad categories to sort the desk's contents (baseball cards in one container, CDs in another, school supplies in a third).

- **Do not get distracted** by schoolwork and other items you come across. If you start questioning your child about a failed test you discover or some questionable reading material you find in a drawer, you will: (1) not get the job done, (2) lose the trust you've started to build with your child, and (3) guarantee that your child will never want to do this with you again. Hand all papers directly to your kid without even looking at them. She can sort through them, categorize them, and throw out the ones she doesn't need anymore.

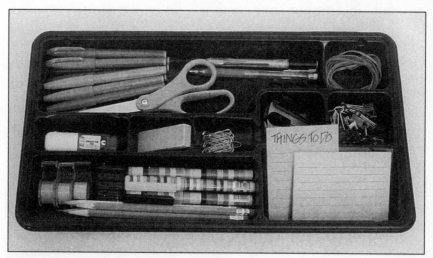

Desk drawer organizer with supplies.

- **Clean the empty drawers** by vacuuming or washing them out.
- **Organize one drawer at a time.** I like to start with the top drawer. Once it is cleaned out, you can place a divided tray in it for supplies. Organize additional drawers as time permits. Refer to the list of suggested drawer categories below.
- **Clean up.** You don't want all of your hard work to go to waste by leaving neat piles on the floor to be destroyed before your next session. Twenty minutes before your determined end time, start to clean up. Gather all of the items that have not yet been properly stored and place them in a desk drawer that hasn't been organized, on an empty bookshelf, or in a box or shopping bag. Mark the drawer, shelf, or bag "In Progress." Keep like items together when you store them if you can; it will save time later.
- **Set up another time to meet.** Be as specific as you can and stick to your commitment. Aim to meet again within the week; you want to keep the momentum going, and you want the desk to be user-friendly as soon as possible.
- **Help your child maintain her desk** by doing a quick cleanup with her in a couple of weeks. It should take between ten and twenty minutes. Do this with her until it becomes a practice she can maintain on her own.

Suggested Drawer Categories

Depending on the number of drawers available and the number of categories you come upon while sorting through the contents of a desk, your child's drawers may include any of the following categories:

- **Often used supplies** (pens and pencils, stapler, staples, ruler, hole punch, calculator, correction fluid, tape, paper clips, sticky notes)
- **Extra school supplies** (loose-leaf paper, printer paper, spiral notebooks, folders, dividers, report and book covers)
- **Art supplies** (No matter what age the student, she will always need markers, colored pencils, poster board, etc., for school projects)
- **Computer supplies** (disks, CDs, extra cables, extra ink cartridges, instruction manuals)
- **Electronics** (portable music player, CDs, video games, camera, film)
- **Collections** (stickers, keychains, stationery, photographs)
- **Junk** (Because every house has a junk drawer and every kid should have one too)

QUICK TIP

Cut out the label from your printer's ink cartridge box and attach it to the bottom of the computer supply drawer, or to the side of the computer, printer, or desk, so you'll always know what type of ink the printer uses.

The Wandering Worker

Whether it's because they like to be near others when they work, or because they do their best thinking lying down, some kids will still choose to forgo their desks for just about any other area in the house. While working at a desk is ideal, a child can get her work done pretty much anywhere if she has what she needs. In order to avoid the constant, distracting search for supplies, create a *portable office* with your child. Whether she likes to do homework at the kitchen table, on the floor, or on a bed, the portable office will allow her to focus on her homework instead of on searching for pencils and glue sticks.

Action: Setting Up the Portable Office

GATHER SUPPLIES

- A tackle box or art supply box with enough compartments to house several different supplies in a way that they can be easily found and put back. Make sure that it latches shut securely.
- Supplies your child needs when she does her homework, such as:
  - Pens and pencils
  - Pencil sharpener
  - Correction fluid and erasers

- Crayons, markers, colored pencils
- Stapler, staples, staple remover
- Tape, glue
- Scissors
- Index cards
- Paper clips
- Ruler
- Calculator
- Highlighters
- Sticky notes
- Hole punch
- Reinforcements
- Compass, protractor

ASSEMBLE THE PORTABLE OFFICE

- **Fill the tackle box or art supply bin with school supplies** together with your child.
- **Explain the importance of making sure the office is packed up** when homework is completed.
- **Show your child that she can work anywhere in the house as long as she has her portable office.** ("Anywhere in the house" may be a relative term—tell your child what rooms are off-limits before she sets herself up on the Persian rug with her Magic Markers.)

HOW LONG WILL THIS TAKE?

Once you've gathered the supplies, it should take between ten and twenty minutes to assemble the portable office.

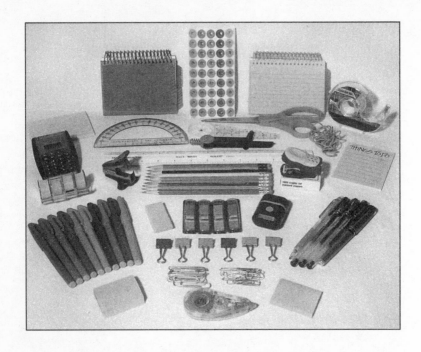

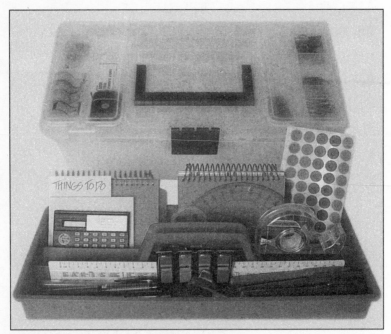

The portable office: supplies and setup.

- **Establish a special place for the portable office** to live so that your child doesn't waste valuable time searching for it before she begins her homework.

LOOSE ENDS

It's important to note that children who tend to work in several locations are children who tend to leave papers behind. Create a *loose paper basket* or *tray* that lives wherever a child does her homework. Stray papers can be gathered in a single spot and then transferred back to her room. Even if the papers don't make it back to the bedroom, at least your child will know where to find her missing math homework.

If your child works in more than one place, set up more than one paper tray. For example, put one in the kitchen and another in the living room if she regularly works in both places. If more than one family member works at a central location, such as at a computer cart, set up a multitiered letter tray or assign each family member his or her own basket. Clearly label each tray or basket so that anyone can match a piece of paper with its owner. Set a limit on how full a tray can get before it needs to be emptied. You will have to oversee the process until it's integrated into the household routine.

Good Work

By implementing the methods described in chapters 3 through 6 you will complete the bulk of your child's physical organization. You should see changes immediately; papers have a home, supplies can be found easily, and homework can be handed in on time. As you move to the next phase of the organizing process continue to reinforce the systems you've set up. Focus on your child's success and she will be encouraged to follow your lead.

CHAPTER 7

Understanding Time Management: The Basics

Now that your child's paper is under control we can move on to the less tangible aspect of organization: **time management.** Time management refers to the ability to prioritize commitments and schedule them with enough time to complete everything satisfactorily. In order to do this one must have both a clear concept of time as well as an ability to accurately gauge how long things take: *What does an hour feel like and how much can I really accomplish in that time?* Time management also requires a person to take into account all of the unexpected things that can interfere with even the most carefully planned schedules. For a student, this means learning to estimate how long his homework and other commitments take, and learning to take sick days, quizzes, and long-term assignments into account so that he has enough of a cushion to complete his work.

Unfortunately, time management is not part of the school curriculum. In fact, many adults still feel like they're playing catch-up for the same reason that so many students feel left behind: no one ever taught them how to manage their time. This is a basic skill that should be taught just like reading, writing, and arithmetic. While school teaches students how to *tell* time, it does not teach them how to *manage* it. Many children can tell you that it's 12:30 and time for lunch, but they cannot gauge how long it will take them to eat or how much time they have left before the next class begins, just as many adults know what time an appointment is, but don't leave enough time to get there or forget to account for traffic.

Most adults actually have the skill of the average third grader when it comes to understanding time. By the age of nine, our education in the field of time is effectively over; once you can distinguish between the big hand and the little hand, you're on your own. You may not have the opportunity to learn time management skills until your company hires a corporate consultant to teach you and your colleagues how to increase efficiency through time management. Employers make the investment because they understand that time is money; if they can train their employees to do more work in less time the company will profit. If we as parents and teachers are willing to make that same investment in our children, imagine how much *they* will profit, both in school and beyond.

The Struggle Today

There are two reasons today's students are struggling with the concept of time even more than students did in past generations. The first is that children today are being taught to tell time at an earlier age. What used to be taught in the second and third grades is now being introduced as early as kindergarten. Most children, however, are not developmentally ready to understand the idea of time at the age of five. In spite of the fact that many children don't grasp the concept, once it's taught, whether it's in first grade or in third, the class moves on. If your child didn't internalize the lessons, he's out of luck, and things only become more challenging as he grows older. In her book *About Dyslexia,* Priscilla Vail describes the far-reaching effects of this educational gap. "Students whose concepts of time and space are blurred will have trouble with the sequence of daily tasks; moving themselves and their materials to different classrooms, and shifting their thinking from one subject matter to another." Without a firm grounding in the practice of time management, students will be challenged throughout school and into the workplace.

The second reason children are struggling more now is that they've grown up in the age of the digital clock. Kids today see time as static numbers displayed on VCRs, microwaves, and alarm clocks instead of as moving hands on analog clocks. Time appears on a digital clock as a statement of "now." It says nothing about the past or future and it doesn't place the present time in the context of the hour or the day. *When time has no context, it has no appreciable meaning.* Conversely, an analog clock with a numbered face and moving hands shows the present time in relation to the past and future (before the hour and after the hour) and is broken down into increments (hours, minutes, and seconds) that work together to create a whole picture. This difference has a huge impact on how children perceive time and on their ability to locate themselves within it.

Children who have grown up with digital clocks have a difficult time finding meaning in the concept of time. Because they cannot picture what a specific measurement of time looks like they cannot translate the numbers on a digital clock into a unit of time they can relate to or manipulate. To them, fifteen minutes is simply a number and not an amount (like a quarter of an hour) or an image (like one fourth of a clock face). Their understanding of time has no depth or movement, and they do not see time in relative terms, which makes it hard to gauge how long things take and to plan realistically.

The Language of Time

"Because time itself is invisible," writes Vail, "the only way to understand it is through language." We employ language to teach the concept of time and to operate within time every day. Words such as *before, after, later, long ago,* and *once upon a time* serve as verbal cues that create a time frame. Together with *yesterday, today,* and *tomorrow,* they serve a dual purpose, referring to specific periods of time while introducing the broader concepts of past, present, and future. The language of time allows us to establish a context in which we can communicate with each other. If your child doesn't recognize the meaning or significance of basic key words, he will have trouble locating things in time. This will make it difficult for him to prioritize and approach his workload efficiently. Vail explains further:

> "When such words as *until, whenever, after, next,* or *ago* don't carry meaning, [children] ignore them in conversation and reading, and these students don't develop a grid of time to organize their learning. Because the language of time isn't part of their thinking, they remain in the present tense, cutting themselves off from the ability to sequence. This makes serious trouble in reading comprehension, writing, understanding literature and history, not to mention planning for long-term assignments. Yet, because the misunderstanding of time is as invisible as the concept itself, the confusion often goes unnoticed and uncorrected."

What makes teaching time management particularly challenging is the fact that it is difficult, if not impossible, to identify a child who is struggling with it. When a parent or teacher sees a student having trouble with math, steps can be taken to accommodate or remediate him. Kids who don't understand time, however, are usually overlooked and don't get the help they need. All through school they have difficulty meeting deadlines and completing their work. They are constantly rushing, often late, and frequently unprepared. As adults they continue to experience the same challenges but now with far greater consequences, since careers often hang in the balance. Their lack of time management skills often means they have difficulty meeting deadlines because they don't account for interruptions or properly gauge how long things are going to take. They can't get to work on time, they forget appointments, and they can often be found rushing from one activity to the next. Without an understanding of time and how to manage it, success in school and in the workplace can be a fruitless and frustrating pursuit. Once the issue is identified, however, it can be addressed, and students and adults alike can reconstruct their perceptions of and approach to time.

Teaching Time

When I teach students about time I break the concept down into the following four areas:

- Telling time
- Weekly time
- Monthly time
- Weekly time for the household

TELLING TIME

To begin this phase of the organizing process, I first get a sense of how well a student understands time. I also want to be sure he knows things as elementary as the sequence of days and months. I want him to be able to quickly associate a month with its corresponding number so he can calculate how much time he has before his next paper is due. These concepts have to be so fluid he doesn't have to think about them. Once he can tell time quickly he can go on to the next level of higher-order thinking without worrying about the basics.

I often determine that a student needs to relearn the concept of time. The first thing you need to do is find out whether or not your child can tell time. I don't mean whether he can read the numbers off the microwave; I mean, does he understand that 6:45 is the same thing as a quarter to seven, or that 10:38 is about twenty to eleven? As I mentioned earlier, digital clocks only reflect the time at a given moment. If your child doesn't associate the number he sees with a bigger picture, he can't grasp the true nature of time.

The first steps towards making time real for your child are to put an analog clock up in your home and to get him an analog watch. He needs to see time move and not just "appear." Using an analog clock will force him to see time in a different way, both literally and figuratively. It may take a while for him to adjust, but it's the best way to learn. When you give your child a watch don't let it seem like a punishment for his failure to grasp the concept of time. Instead, turn it into a gift

An analog watch, an analog clock with a timer, and the Time-Timer.

he'll enjoy using. Give him one of your own old watches or let him pick out one he likes. When you approach this as a positive experience, your child will be more open to it.

If your child is a visual learner, the Time-Timer is a tool that can help make time real. Its appearance is similar to that of a clock, but it's numbered in one-minute increments and counts down from sixty minutes to zero. When the time is set, the designated amount of time is represented by a red section that grows smaller as time passes. This tool trains your child to recognize time passing and to judge how long he has left to complete a task by showing him how much time has elapsed and how much time remains. Its similarity to a clock allows your child to transfer what he learns to any analog watch or clock. You may want to pair it with a standard timer that is set to ring when the time is up in order to add an audio cue.

Exercises for Teaching Time

Take the lessons out of the academic world and bring them into a world that interests your child. Come up with interesting ways to give your child an accurate sense of time. Don't hound him about it and don't make it a chore. Simply try to engage him in something that involves keeping track of time. The aim is to put the power in his hands and let him learn through experience. Here are some ideas to start you off:

- Use an analog watch with a second hand to time your child and ask him to tell you when he thinks one minute is up. When he's done, give him the watch and let him do the same for you. It will probably surprise both of you to see how long a minute really lasts. Then show your child how to count each second in increments of "one-one hundred, two-one hundred, three-one hundred" and time each other again. See how close you can each get to a full minute.

- Have your child learn to gauge time by experimenting with things he's already familiar with. Be creative! Here are a few examples:
  - How many (sit-ups, lists of comic book heroes, names of favorite movies) can you do/come up with in a minute?
  - How long is your favorite song?
  - What's your best time on a video game?
  - How fast can you race to the corner and back?
- Give your child a "job." Tell him you're working hard on a project and would like him to let you know when five minutes has passed, or ask him to remind you in half an hour that you have to call Grandma.

THINK ABOUT IT

Without realizing it parents often give their children an inaccurate sense of time. Think about the last time you told your child you were leaving the house in five minutes. How long did that five minutes really last? When five minutes turns into twenty, your child gains an extra fifteen minutes for himself but loses any sense of what five minutes really means.

House Rules

You may or may not have rules in your home about how much time your child is allowed to spend watching TV or playing video games, but it's always a good idea to make sure you both know how long things actually take. You may find that for your child a typical video game lasts about five minutes, in which case playing three games a night could be a reasonable break from homework. On the other hand, you may discover that each game takes fifteen minutes. If your child repeatedly begs for "just one more game" he can end up spending hours playing video games instead of doing homework! If this is the case you may want to rephrase your video-game policy so that your child has a time limit instead of a number of games he's allowed to play.

Figure out together how much time your child spends on nonacademic activities such as video games, Internet surfing, e-mail, instant messaging, and talking on the phone. Then decide on a time limit for each. A standard timer can be a useful tool (but again, don't hound him with it); it can help him stick to his plan and decide where he wants to spend his time.

Calendar Time versus Study Time

Kids don't think past the end of the day, and "right now" is their usual frame of reference. They don't think long-term, which makes it hard for them to plan realistically. When students are younger, teachers break down everything for them, from the daily routine to homework assignments. In middle school teachers assume that students have the ability to do this on their own and no longer monitor the class so closely. Depending on a student's age and level of development, however, he may not be a good predictor of time, and this will have significant impact on his ability to succeed in school.

If a student is unable to gauge how long an assign ment will take he will probably not leave enough time to complete it. In addition, most students have an unclear picture of what has to be done on a daily, weekly, and monthly basis. They don't see what needs to be finished when, and they don't distinguish between the number of days on their calendar and the amount of time actually available for schoolwork. This can easily lead to missed assignments and disappointing grades.

Aisha, a high school junior, was a high-ranked amateur tennis player with an active social life. All of her afternoons and many weekends involved tennis practice or games, and her downtime was usually spent with friends. School was not a priority for her, and between her rigorous schedule and her lack of organizational skills her grades were suffering. While Aisha considered school incidental and didn't particularly care about her grades, her parents felt differently.

When I was called in to help, I found that it wasn't too hard to get Aisha physically organized; the real difficulty I encountered was her inability to gauge time. We met in the early fall, a few weeks before Thanksgiving. She had two papers due within the next month and a half, a science paper and a critical thinking paper for her English class, each of which involved a few hundred pages of reading. Aisha was confident that she could easily finish her work by the deadline, but I wasn't so sure she had an accurate picture of how much time she really had. I was not, however, going to tell her this. It wasn't going to help Aisha to hear the conclusions I had come to—she had to draw her own.

Parents tend to give their kids answers instead of allowing them to figure out their own solutions. Students need to discover and solve their own problems. The solution a child comes up with herself is the one that's going to stick; my job was to lead Aisha down the path towards self-discovery by asking questions that would allow her to come up with answers that made sense to her.

It was clear that Aisha's schedule was packed. Tennis practice kept her after school every day, which meant she didn't get home until seven or eight and rarely started her homework before eight-thirty. This allowed her only enough time to complete that day's assignments and left no room to work on long-term projects during the week. In addition, Aisha informed me that she was always exhausted by the end of the week, so she never did schoolwork on Fridays; she liked to reserve Saturdays for socializing when she didn't have a tennis tournament; her brother was coming home from college that weekend, and she planned to hang out with him; and Thanksgiving was just around the corner, and she had no intentions of doing schoolwork over the holiday break.

At this point I took out a calendar. We crossed out every block of time during which Aisha had declared herself unavailable, which included all weekdays, Friday nights, days that featured tennis tournaments, and special events. When we were finished Aisha was left with *eight days out of forty-five* to read four hundred and seventy pages and write two papers. She was stunned. We then calculated that if the writing was going to take three days, that would leave five days for reading, which translated into almost a hundred pages a day. Aisha, who was not a fast reader, turned to me, terrified. "I can't do it!" This was the "a-ha!" moment I had been waiting for.

When her panic subsided, I reassured Aisha that she could certainly meet her deadlines, we just had to figure out how. The next step was to guide her to find the solution that would fit her life. Aisha took another look at the calendar,

ANALYSIS

■ I knew right away that Aisha wouldn't have enough time to get her two papers done if she stuck to her typical schedule, but she needed to discover that for herself. If I had told her my impression when we started she would have shut me out immediately—as soon as kids hear negative talk they stop listening. The only way to have an impact is to let them go through the process themselves so that they can come up with their own conclusions and solutions.

■ Six weeks of calendar time does not translate into six weeks of available work time. Give your child the tools she needs to understand the logistics of her schedule and then let her make choices about how to best allocate her time.

■ Encourage your child to look for creative *but realistic* ways to find time to get her work done. This part will involve some trial and error, but the best way for your child to learn is through experience.

knowing she needed to find several more hours a week to devote to her long-term assignments. She had a fairly large number of nonnegotiable commitments and knew she would have to be creative about finding extra time. For example, she had never studied on the bus to and from tournaments, but she now realized that these were valuable hours that could be spent catching up on her reading. She also decided to do some work when her brother was home visiting and to cut back somewhat on socializing over the weekend. And, finally, she realized she could gain a couple of days by working over Thanksgiving weekend. Now that she had an accurate sense of her available time and commitments Aisha was able to make choices that allowed her to follow her passions and, at the same time, get her work done.

CHAPTER 8

Making Time Work: The Planner

A student who understands how to use time to her advantage has an accurate picture of her weekly schedule and a realistic sense of her commitments. She is aware of upcoming tests and deadlines, she knows how to break down long-term assignments, and she can balance her life. A student who is not equipped with such skills will pull a lot of all-nighters and miss a lot of deadlines.

To help students manage their time effectively I use a planner, a tool that makes time visible and tangible. It captures activities, assignments, and deadlines in one place while your child learns to grasp the ever-elusive concept of time. The planner allows a student to:

- Keep track of immediate deadlines and long-term projects
- Keep track of both her academic and personal lives
- Gauge how long things take
- Calculate how much time she has to complete her work
- Block out study time in her schedule

- See the tasks she needs to accomplish on a daily and weekly basis, all in one place

Time management is about incorporating all of the elements of one's life into a schedule that accommodates everything, and the planner is designed to help students do just that. Its format allows your child to see her assignments *in context*. They can be viewed in relation to each other and in relation to the other things she has to accomplish. Because everything is laid out clearly on a grid, your child can tell immediately when she's going to have a conflict, whether it's two tests on the same day or a basketball game the night before a paper is due. Armed with this information she can plan accordingly. When a student tries to keep all of this information in her head, she can't see the overlap in location, time, or events. She doesn't realize until it's too late that she has left herself fifteen minutes to get somewhere that's half an hour away or that all of her midsemester deadlines fall within three days of each other.

The information in the planner is arranged so that a student can quickly see how much work she has in a given class and on a given night. If she looks at the row designated for "history" she can see how much reading she has to do for the week, as well as whether she has any tests or papers coming up. If she glances down the column under Monday and every box is full, she knows she has a lot of homework Monday night. When a student uses the planner consistently she often starts to see patterns in the way teachers run their classrooms. One teacher may give quizzes every Friday and another may assign homework that's always due on Tuesday. When a stu-

subjects   binder   Tuesday's home-   colored flags signal upcoming   weekend
            clip   work in all subjects tests and deadlines   schedule

tracking
homework
and study
time for a
single sub-
ject through-
out the week

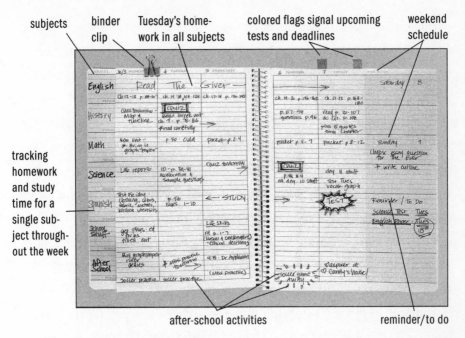

after-school activities   reminder/to do

Sample planner page.

dent can predict a teacher's behavior, she can account for it
when she plans her homework and study schedule.

Accounting for Time Out of School

In order for a student to realistically manage her time she
has to see her work in relation to her other commitments.
After-school activities clearly affect how much free time a student has, which directly affects how much time she can spend
on schoolwork. The last row in the planner, designated "After
School," gives your child an immediate picture of any possible
conflicts with studying and schoolwork, from hockey practice
to doctors' appointments. By taking all of these different

events into account, she learns to see her life as a whole instead of in isolated compartments. When she sees how one element relates to another she can make informed choices that reflect her priorities.

In order for the planner to be an effective tool kids have to record all of their after-school activities consistently. They hate to do this. I don't really blame them—it's dull work to list a year's worth of chorus rehearsals. But if they don't write down their activities, they don't see them. And if they don't see them, they don't take them into account when planning their work schedules. If your child has a piano lesson every Tuesday she may argue that she's not going to forget about it so she shouldn't have to write it down. Tell her that it's not that you expect her to forget, it's that she has to see it in her planner so she can plan around it when preparing for long-term deadlines, tests, and quizzes.

THINK ABOUT IT

Often the busier you are, the more you accomplish. Don't think that eliminating an after-school sport or activity will make your child do her homework. Instead, help her create a balanced schedule that accommodates the things she wants to do and leaves adequate time for the things she *has* to do.

The filled-in boxes in the planner create a visual pattern that most kids can't recreate in their minds. It won't take long for your child to fill in one month's worth of activities at a time, and it will make a huge difference in her ability to manage her time. If she won't write down the details, she can at least write down what time she expects to be home each day of the week so that she can determine how much time she'll have to complete her homework and whether she'll have additional time to dedicate to long-term projects.

School Planners

Educators know that students need to keep track of assignments and many schools now provide students with planners. Unfortunately, many school-issued planners are not designed with a true understanding of how students think and what they need. The planners are often modeled on adult calendars that show one or two days on a page broken down by the hour or that show one week on two pages listing one day below the next. These formats generally don't work for students. The layouts don't allow kids to see how one day relates to the next or what needs to be accomplished for a single subject within a week.

Adults require different planners because their routines and responsibilities are completely different from those of a student. Adults who are no longer in school usually have just one or two tasks to follow up on at the end of the day whereas students need to reconstruct the entire day in order to be successful in school the next morning. They have to go class by class, period by period to see what needs to be accomplished for each subject. The best way to do that is to see all of the relevant information laid out clearly in one place.

Even when a school provides a well-designed planner, students are often not thoroughly instructed in how to use it. Often educators don't recognize that it is just as important for students to keep track of commitments outside of school as it is to keep track of assignments and deadlines. This step is pivotal not only in helping students keep their extracurricular lives straight but also in giving them an accurate sense of their available time. In addition, the technical aspect of using a planner is usually taught once in the beginning of the year, after which it is assumed that students know what they're doing. I met one student halfway through the school year who could never open his planner to the correct day. When I showed him that he could fold back the page of the completed week so that his planner opened automatically to the current week he was amazed. "So *that's* why all the kids have been folding their pages back! I never understood why they did that." Either he had missed the lesson on how to use the planner or he hadn't picked up on this particular tip.

Hearing something important once is not enough for most kids. All children learn differently and the information doesn't always register the first time. Repetition allows them to incorporate what they're being taught, test their understanding of it, ask questions, and correct mistakes. Some kids, such as those joining a new school after the planner has already been introduced, may never learn how to use their school's planner at all. Making an investment in a planner means making an investment of time; teaching students how to use it is as important as providing the tool.

Making the Change

Your child may take to the planner right away. Remember Natalie, the sixth grader who was having trouble making the transition from lower school to middle school, whose dad followed her to her locker to search for her missing homework? The planner was the tool that put control back in her hands. It gave her something tangible to rely on and helped her adjust to the changes she was facing in school. It took her longer to master her paper flow, just as some students take longer to make use of the planner. In fact, Natalie's immediate adoption of the planner is the exception rather than the rule. Even though it's the pivotal step in a student's organizing system it's usually the last one to fall into place. Because it's more challenging to understand and maintain than paper flow systems, the planner is the last step I introduce. There are several reasons why it takes time for students to make the transition into using the planner.

Some kids aren't ready for the responsibility of being accountable for their work. Intellectually they understand that the planner makes sense, but they aren't emotionally ready to face what they have to do. I worked with Louis, a high school sophomore, who once admitted to me that when he used the planner it was great, but as soon as he started feeling overwhelmed he stopped using it. Something about writing the assignments down made him feel accountable for the work, and when he was feeling anxious about school, he didn't want to face what he had to do. If he didn't write the homework down, it didn't exist. I accepted that this was something Louis had to work out for himself, and I didn't push him. The following year he felt ready to commit to using his planner, and his grades quickly improved. He became so devoted to the planner that when he lost it halfway through the semester, he called me immediately to replace it. No one is perfect; at least if your child has systems in place that work for him, he can reconstruct them if he has to.

Other students don't want to look different from their classmates or insist that they're only allowed to use their school-issued planners. In either of these situations I tear out a few pages from my planner and ask the student to try using the system for a couple of weeks just to see if it works. If the child is younger I ask her if she'd like her parents to speak to the teacher about using a different planner; parents can intervene if the child agrees. Almost all teachers are accommodating. They are generally less concerned with the type of planner being used than with the fact that it's being used at all. When a teacher sees a student handing in her homework and performing well in school, she's unlikely to push her to give up a system that's working.

Still other students resist the planner because they are convinced that they can keep all of the information in their heads. These students are often very smart and usually *can* retain a lot of information. But there will come a time when it's simply too much to hold on to; a student will miss a deadline or forget about a test, and her system will come crashing down. It is, of course, difficult to convince her of this. If this is your child, my best advice is to give it time. When other pieces of the system fall into place she will probably be willing to give the planner a shot.

And then there are the students who see the planner as an extra step they simply don't want to deal with. They find it boring and repetitive or don't want to bother pulling out an extra book to write down their homework. I leave them alone until they're ready to take on the planner or to at least try it for a couple of weeks. In my experience, students who are willing to try the planner for a couple of weeks discover its value and abandon their old homework pads. Students have told me that while their paper flow systems have helped them improve their performance in school, they know that they would have been even more successful if they had used the planner sooner. They would have started projects earlier and not left everything for the last minute, or seen that they were about to be bombarded in school and been able to prepare for it. In general, when a student sees that using the planner consistently leads to better grades, less stress, and more free time, she is willing to invest in the process.

Most students start using the planner when they mature emotionally and/or intellectually. Like all systems I introduce, however, the planner is effective only if a student is willing to use it. Some kids find value in the planner but, for one reason or another, stop using it. It may be that they're overwhelmed like Louis, or that they're simply exhausted. There is usually a correlation between the state of a student's planner and the time of year. Just before school holidays there's generally a drop in how consistently students write in their planners. Everyone's wiped out. The students who generally do well in school are tired, and the ones who experience more academic difficulty are often doing twice as much work just trying to keep themselves together. Planners are frequently empty by the end of the year. Remember that time management and the planner are not about being perfect; all students have good weeks and bad weeks. These are simply tools to add to your child's collection so that she can discover what works best for her.

Modalities

Use different modalities when you teach your child about the planner. The planner is a visual tool that incorporates color and creates a visual representation of your child's workload and schedule. For the child who is stronger in auditory learning, use language to break down each of the visual elements and talk her through each step of the process. For the kinesthetic learner, make sure she manipulates the planner herself, assembles it, and writes in it while you're explaining it to her. Using different modalities together is the best way to ensure that your child understands what you're teaching her.

How Much Time Does Your Child Really Have?

To gain an accurate sense of how much time she really has, your child has to account for everything in her schedule and then learn how to gauge how long things really take. Among the things students should learn to consider when creating a schedule are:

- Social life and special events
- Travel time
- Research

- Assembly of the final project (including clean-up time, spell checking, adding visuals, and printing the final paper)
- Delays beyond one's control (e.g., the library doesn't have the book she needs and it has to be shipped from another branch)

Your child should make a habit of expecting the unexpected and planning for it. If she assumes something is going to come up that will interfere with her schedule or deadline, she can leave extra time to accommodate the delays and interruptions. When a student tells me she plans to finish a long-term assignment the day before it's due I tell her she's not expecting the unexpected. Sometime before the due date something will come up and steal time that was supposed to be spent on the assignment—an unexpected quiz, a stomachache, a bad day. Whatever it is, if she hasn't built in a cushion of time, she's not going to get her work done the way she wanted to.

THINK ABOUT IT

Your child can practice gauging time by predicting how long she expects to spend on homework for each subject on a specific night and writing the estimates in her planner. As she completes each assignment, she can compare her guess with how long the work actually took her. It's likely that she'll find that most assignments took twice as long as she expected. She should try this once every couple of weeks and see if her estimates improve.

Assessment Questions

To help determine how your child keeps track of her schoolwork and other commitments

- *Does your child's school require a specific planner?*

- *Where does your child record her assignments?*
    a. In a school-designated planner
    b. In a planner you purchased at the beginning of the year
    c. In an undated pad of paper
    d. On random pages in her binder or notebook
    e. In her head
    f. Apparently she never has to write down her homework assignments because she always completes them in school.

- *Does your child call classmates every night to find out what her assignments are?*

- *Rate the following in terms of Always, Sometimes, or Never. Your child:*
    a. Doesn't know due dates for assignments
    b. Is surprised by tests and quizzes
    c. Starts big projects the night before they're due
    d. Ask you at 10:00 P.M. for something she needs the next day in school, like brownies for a bake sale or help packing for a class trip you didn't know about

- **If you answered "never"** to most of the statements, then your kid is on top of her game. She will probably take to the planner easily when she sees how effective it is in arranging her schedule and planning her time.

- **If you answered "sometimes"** to two or more of the statements, your child has some strengths and some weaknesses in the area of time management. Applaud the strengths and explore the weaknesses together. The planner will be a very useful tool for keeping all of your child's information in one place and helping her plan ahead.

- **If you answered "always"** to most of the statements, it's likely that your child has little if any understanding of how to manage time. This will be one of the most important chapters for your child. Take your time so that she can incorporate each lesson as she's ready.

To identify patterns in your child's schedule and approach to schoolwork

- *What time does your child get home from school?*

- *What are your child's after-school commitments (broken down season by season)? Include sports (practice sessions and games), music (rehearsals and performances), and other school-related activities; after-school jobs and chores; religious school; and community service.*

  Fall:

  Winter:

  Spring:

Summer:

Yearlong:

- *When does your child do homework during the week?*
  a. Before dinner
  b. After dinner
  c. Both
  d. Before television, computer games, magazine reading, etc.
  e. After television, computer games, magazine reading, etc.
  f. While she's watching television
  g. In the morning, before school
  h. In school, during study hall
  i. In class, right before the teacher collects it

- *When does your child do homework over the weekend?*
  a. Friday afternoons
  b. Saturdays
  c. Saturday nights
  d. Sundays
  e. Sunday night, as late as possible
  f. Never
  g. It varies every weekend.

- *When does your child work on long-term assignments?*
  a. During the school week
  b. Only on weekends
  c. Throughout the week and on weekends, whenever she can find time
  d. She starts them the night before they're due.

- *Is your child a slow, average, or fast reader?*

- *Can your child pull off an A project the night before it's due?*

- *Does your child ask you for help with schoolwork at the last minute?*

- *Does your child call you from school asking you to drop off her homework/textbook/science project/lunch because she left it at home?*

Action: Setting Up the Planner

The planner is set up in a specific way, using a particular plan book and a well-defined format. It corresponds to a student's binder or accordion file and desktop file box in both color and sequence. It's important to follow the guidelines here as closely as possible. Of course, there is still room for your child to be creative—she can choose colors she likes and decorate the planner in any way that appeals to her.

HOW LONG WILL THIS TAKE?

It should take about forty-five minutes to an hour to set up your child's planner. This includes the physical setup and some practice runs that will help your child see how the planner is used to track both academic and nonacademic activities, as well as short- and long-term assignments.

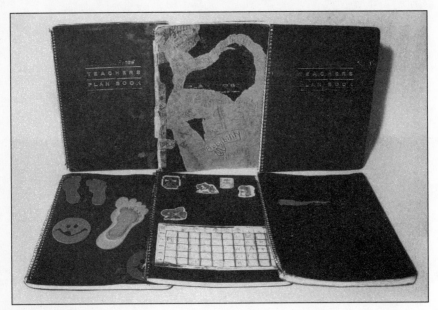

Sample planner covers.

GATHER SUPPLIES

- A teacher's planner (seven- or ten-subject, depending on your child's curriculum)
- Colored markers
- Small set(s) of colored sticky flags (they usually come in packs of five; you will need one color for each class)
- A small binder clip
- A pencil and eraser
- Glue or tape
- A copy of your child's class schedule and class syllabi
- Your child's school calendar
- Copies of your child's extracurricular schedule(s)

LAYING OUT THE PLANNER

- **I generally use a standard teacher's planner with seven rows and seven columns.** This accommodates most students' schedules (which typically consist of five subjects). Students with heavier course loads can use plan books with room for up to eight classes or split rows between two classes with little homework.

- **List your child's subjects** in the left column of the first week. Use colors that correspond to the subject colors in the paper flow system and desktop file box. (If your child's history file is red, write "history" in red in the planner.)

- **Leave two empty boxes** in the first column after you've filled in the subjects. Label the first with the name of your child's school. This row will be used to list anything she needs to remember that isn't subject specific, such as getting a permission slip signed, returning a library book, or meeting a teacher for a conference.

- **Label the bottom box** "After School," "Other," "P.M.," or any other name your child likes that reflects her after-school schedule. This row will be used to record all extracurricular activities, including team practices and games, doctors' appointments, social events, and lessons.

- **Fill in the calendar dates** (weekly and daily) at the top of each page. Do this for two months' worth of classes (or more), using a school calendar as a guide. Be sure to label vacation days as well.

- **Divide the remaining space** on the right page between

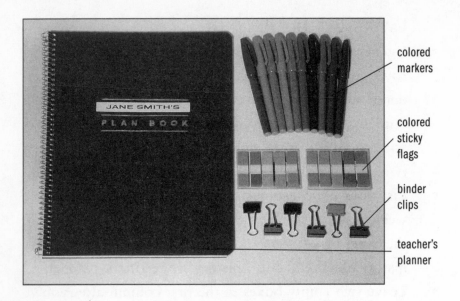

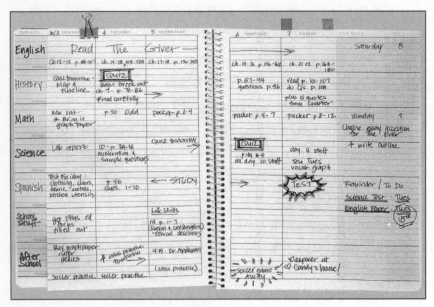

The Planner: supplies and setup.

"Saturday" "Sunday," and "Reminder/To Do" if your planner does not include these sections.

- **Tear out a few extra pages** from the back of the planner for your child to keep in her binder or accordion file. These pages can be used as backup to record homework if she forgets or misplaces her planner.

How to Use the Planner

DAILY HOMEWORK

- Your child should write down each homework assignment *on the day it is given* (as opposed to the day it is due).
- Each assignment is recorded in the *column of the day* and the *row of the subject*. For example, your child should be able to read a week's worth of English assignments from left to right.

LONG-TERM ASSIGNMENTS

- Tests, quizzes, and major deadlines are recorded on the day they're announced. At home that evening your child should transfer the information to the *due date* or *test date*. If the due date is later than the current week, she should *flag* it at the top of the page with a sticky flag in the color that coordinates with the subject (for example, if "history" is written in red, use a red flag). The sticky flag should stick out at the top of the planner, reminding her of the upcoming deadline.

week one:
read book

week two:
write essay
1st draft
rewrite
complete
& print
week
three:
essay due

flag
indicates
deadline

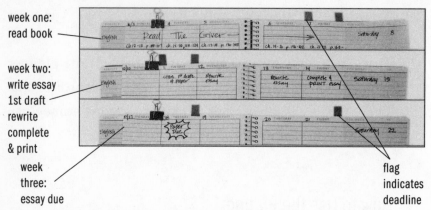

Long-term assignment broken down by task and due date.

- The next stage in approaching long-term assignments, tests, or quizzes is to break down the steps needed to prepare for the deadline and assign smaller deadlines to each step. Once this is done your child can record those deadlines in the planner.
- Your child should check her deadlines along the way. If she's on schedule, great; if not, she has to play catch-up to get to the next due date or compute new deadlines, depending on where she is in the process and how much extra time she has.

RULE OF THUMB

Subtract two days for every week assigned to a project and make that the deadline. For example, if a paper is assigned on a Monday and due in two weeks, your child should subtract four days and aim to complete the paper by the previous Thursday. This creates a cushion in case other things come up that interfere with her work.

- When the week is complete, your child will *turn the page and fold the first column back* so the subject names on page one are visible. This way the subjects need to be listed only once instead of being rewritten each week.
- Your child should *fasten the folded pages together with the binder clip* on the left side so that she can open immediately to the current week in her planner.

After-School Activities and Special Events

- **Ongoing after-school activities.** Use your child's team, club, or committee schedule(s) to record upcoming games, practice sessions, meetings, and other activities in the planner. Your child should record regular extracurricular meetings (club meetings, rehearsals) on a weekly or monthly basis and special events (school dances, family get-togethers) when the information comes in (on invitations, announcements, or fliers).
- **Invitations and special events.** Once the date and time of an event has been recorded in your child's planner and in your own calendar or in the family calendar, the actual invitation, flier, or schedule should be filed in your child's desktop file box, assuming the event applies specifically to her. This way everyone knows about the upcoming event, and the details (like directions or attire) can be quickly and easily accessed when needed. This is an im-

portant step towards taking the responsibility for such events out of your hands and putting it in your child's. If she consistently depends on you for reminders and information, she won't learn to rely on herself. Now that she has a safe place to keep information until she's ready to retrieve it, it should be her job to take care of it.

- **Family events.** If the family makes plans, pass the information on to your child so that she can record it in her planner and take it into account when she views her schedule. You should hold on to the actual invitation and transfer the information to your child in a written format (instead of verbally). Jot down the relevant details on a sticky note and put it someplace she's sure to see it. If she finds the note on her computer or desk she will be able to write it into her planner easily; if you shout the information out to her as she's running out the door, it's never going to make it into the planner.

CHAPTER 9

Big-Picture Planning: Electronic, Monthly, and Household

Successful time management requires an awareness of how details fit within a bigger picture. While the planner allows your child to keep track of both, there are additional tools that can help you and your child focus on individual aspects of time management in greater depth. These tools include electronic tracking systems, monthly calendars for students, and weekly calendars for households.

Electronic Trends

Advances in technology have brought about two trends that affect the way students keep track of their schedules and assignments. The first trend is the proliferation of the personal digital assistant (PDA). Some students use them effectively, but my experience has been that most kids abandon them within a relatively short period of time. The small size of the PDA screen prohibits students from viewing a week's worth of assignments and activities at a time, which is what most kids need to do in order to create a realistic study schedule. If they synchronize their PDAs with their computers every day they can view the information on a larger screen, but most kids don't take the time for this step. Even those who want to don't always find it convenient to do so, and they end up with a limited picture of what they have to do. Other factors that make the PDA a less than ideal tool for students include dying batteries, complicated alphabets, the length of time it takes to turn on the PDA and get to the right screen, and the fact that it's a lot more expensive to replace a PDA than a planner.

The second trend is that many schools are taking advantage of current technology to post homework and weekly syllabi online. Electronic posting ensures that both students and parents know about upcoming deadlines and assignments, but the downside is that it lessens your child's accountability. When he is no longer required to keep track of assignments and deadlines himself, he loses out. He misses the opportunity to absorb important information by writing it down, loses training in a skill he's going to need throughout his life, and does not create an overview of what needs to get done. Posting homework online eliminates the planner, which eliminates the big picture. When schools post homework online, it's extremely difficult to justify asking a student to copy all of his homework assignments into his planner. I don't blame a kid for not wanting to recopy it, but seeing how the different parts of the day interact is a huge part of being able to plan successfully. If your child can't understand the value of transferring the postings into his planner, look for other ways to help him view all of his responsibilities at once. Here are a few good options:

- Have your child print each class's assignments and syllabi off the school's Web site so that he can look at everything together.

- Ask your child to track the big things, like long-term assignments and tests, in the planner so they don't get lost in the shuffle. He can record just the basic information about daily assignments ("math sheet," "English essay," "lab report") in his planner so he can predict how much time he will have left for long-term work.

- Have your child track long-term assignments on his *monthly calendar* (described below) and use his planner to record estimates of how long he thinks each regular assignment will take him every night. If he still resists writing down the estimate, he can at least come up with an estimate in his head. It's a start. He can then gauge how long that night's work will take him and determine whether he has time to work on long-term projects that night in addition to his daily assignments.

Monthly Planning for the Student

Once students begin to manage their time week by week, they can move on to looking at their commitments for the month. A monthly calendar will broaden a student's view of the future. A small calendar (8½" x 11") can be hung over the

a monthly calendar can be hung over the front of the desktop file box

Monthly calendar tracks important deadlines and events.

front of the desktop file box so that it will be easily visible. If the file box doesn't fit on the desk, the calendar can be hung on a bulletin board or wall in front of the desk or wherever your child works.

When he is assigned a long-term project, your child should record the deadline in his monthly calendar in addition to marking it in his planner. The next step is to break the project down into the steps needed to arrive at the long-term goal (pick a topic, go to the library, write note cards, complete an outline, write a number of drafts, etc.) and to list individual deadlines for each step on the calendar. The value of a monthly calendar is that it allows a student to see several weeks ahead. Like Aisha, the tennis player, most students have an inaccurate view of how much time they actually have. When a teacher announces that a paper is due in three weeks it seems like an eternity to most kids. If a student can't translate three weeks into twenty-one days and recognize that he will have shorter deadlines within that time period, he thinks he has plenty of time to start his work. If he indicates the deadline on his monthly calendar, however, and then blocks off all the time during which he won't be available to work on the project, he'll suddenly see a very different picture. What looked like a three-week assignment may now be a five-day assignment that demands every available moment before the due date. And even if a student doesn't bother to calculate his time, at least he will see the deadline creeping up on him and will not be surprised by it the night before.

THINK ABOUT IT

When your child is assigned a long-term project does he complete it immediately (within a day or two), even though it's not due for six weeks? It could be that your child is extremely efficient, and it's certainly an excellent habit to start working on long-term projects right away. Generally, however, if a teacher gives a class six weeks to complete an assignment, there's no way it can be done properly in two days. Long-term assignments require significant research, thought, and work in order to produce well-developed results. Check in with your child to make sure he's getting all the information he needs and answering all of the questions he's being asked.

Weekly Planning for the Household: The Organized Home

The planner and student's monthly calendar are tools that will help your child get a handle on his schoolwork and social life. What they won't do is let him know what's going on in the household at large, which is just as important, particularly if he needs your help with something. Many people manage their families and homes with a monthly calendar. This can be efficient for parents, but it doesn't work for kids. Doctors' appointments, family vacations, and after-school activities may all make it onto the calendar, but kids aren't going to check it to see what's coming down the road. Their needs and thoughts are immediate, and learning how to think long-term is a skill that kids develop at different rates. Before they can truly conquer thinking a month in advance, they have to learn to think a week in advance. The Organized Home weekly calendar is designed to help families with children of all ages streamline their schedules, avoid conflicts, and learn about long-term planning. It works the way students think and has been used to avert many a late-night crisis.

The Organized Home is an erasable magnetic calendar. It is kept in a central location, usually on the refrigerator, so that everyone has easy (and frequent) access to it. It is updated every week to reflect the activities of everyone in the household. In addition to keeping track of appointments it can be used to introduce basic concepts of time to younger children. You can review the days of the week and the months of the year, together with their corresponding numbers (**October = the 10th month**) each week when filling in the calendar. Broader concepts like yesterday, today, and tomorrow, and past, present, and future can be introduced and referenced on a regular basis.

The Organized Home also helps family members learn to respect each other's time. One reason we run into scheduling conflicts with our kids is that we often don't tell them when we are and are not available. Particularly now, with more parents working outside of the home, it's important to be clear

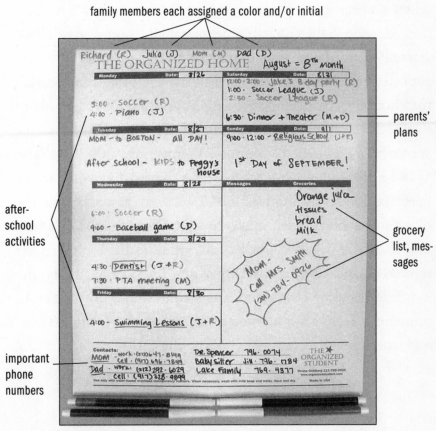

The Organized Home refrigerator magnet.

about when we have time to help out with homework and special projects. When a parent clearly indicates his schedule in a visible place, responsibility is transferred to the child to be accountable for his own time and to know when others are available. Each family member is assigned a color and all relevant information (such as appointments, rehearsals, team practices, and evenings out) is recorded at the beginning of the week, usually by a parent. Once everyone is trained to check the calendar, each person can identify where he or she has to be and when, and know where to find other family members when necessary.

My son Saul came to me one night soon after I had started using the calendar and asked me to help him with a project that was due the next day. He got upset when I told him I had a meeting that night and wouldn't be able to work with him. I took him to the calendar and pointed at the spot where I'd written "Mom—PTA meeting, 7:00" and said, "I'm happy to help you with your projects, but you can see here that I'm not around tonight. I was here yesterday and the day before. Next time, make sure you look at the calendar and then you'll know when I have time to help you." After two weeks of wanting my help when I wasn't available, my kids finally understood that I was serious about my time commitments. They soon learned to be serious about theirs too, and from then on, everyone checked the calendar.

Take Your Time

Introducing your child to the concept and tools of time management is a challenging job. He may not be ready to apply what he learns right away. In fact, you may not see changes in his studying and planning at all. He may pull all-nighters through college before he realizes the value and necessity of these skills. The important thing is that you've started a dialog with your child. You have shown him the path so that when he's ready to go forward your words will echo back to him.

Take it one step at a time. When your child starts to see results he will be more inclined to see the extra effort as a worthwhile investment. This is a long-term process with far-reaching effects. Your child needs to be emotionally and intellectually ready for each stage before you introduce it. It's worth taking the time to make sure your child absorbs the concepts and learns how to apply them.

Although this is the last element of your child's organizing system there is one more step that is an essential part of the process. The next chapter will take you through the end-of-the-year wrap-up which will help your child start the new school year in control and ready to focus on learning.

CHAPTER 10

It's Not Over 'Til It's Over: The End-of-Year Wrap-up

Fantasies of the perfectly organized life almost always involve neatly wrapping up every project. Whether it's a dinner party or a business presentation, the dream is to have all of your materials put away, the trash thrown out, and important information organized and stored properly. Reality, however, is rarely so accommodating. When one task ends you're already in the middle of six others, and new papers, plans, and notes are piling up on top of old ones. If you're lucky you have time to sweep everything related to an old project into a file and shove it someplace out of the way. If you're not so lucky the project becomes another layer on your desk to be excavated at some future date. The wrap-up is the easiest step to abandon because it comes when the event or deadline has passed and other issues seem more pressing, but the consequence of skipping this step is that it is difficult to focus on new projects. Your desk is a mess, you're waiting for loose ends to be tied up, and you can't access information because you never put it away properly.

While closure in your own life is sometimes beyond reach, you can still help your child learn the skills she needs to integrate this habit into her life. When a student learns at an early age that a project, however small, isn't complete until it's wrapped up, she will start to include the step in her planning instead of considering it dispensable or a burden. This will, of course, take some practice—think about how many times throughout your child's early years you had to remind her to brush her teeth, put her dirty clothes in the hamper, or turn out the light when she left a room.

Wrapping Up the School Year

Each completed school year is basically a giant project that needs to be sorted through, purged, organized, and stored so that your child can begin the next school year with a clear desk and a clear mind. Of course, in all my years of coaching I haven't actually met a kid who wants to do this. Spending time with one's class notes once school is over seems above and beyond the call of duty. By June, both you and your child are wiped out, and the last thing either of you want to do is clean out notebooks and files. Kids don't get a great sense of accomplishment from purging and organizing old notes. It's one thing to assemble a new binder that she can use the next day in school, but sorting through last year's homework is fairly anticlimactic; it becomes just one more obstacle between your child and the freedom of summer.

Not only does the wrap-up lay the groundwork for a successful and organized new school year, but it is also an opportunity to preserve your child's memories. You want her to be able to look back in thirty years and enjoy the stories she wrote or laugh at the pictures she drew. A great way to start this process is to bring out some things that were saved from your own childhood or that you may have saved from your child's early school years. Tell her why you value these things and then ask her what she thinks of the memorabilia. Start a discussion about what's worth keeping and why, questions that lie at the heart of this process.

TIMING

Some parents view the summer as an opportunity to thoroughly clean out their children's rooms and closets. That's fine, but you should separate that project from the academic wrap-up and deal with the school materials first. I recommend tackling the wrap-up as soon after school ends as possible. Give your child a day or two to decompress, but catch her before she disappears into the summer. If your child plans to use her backpack for camp or other summer activities, go through it together instead of letting her dump the contents on the floor where they'll stay for the next two months. If there's absolutely no time to do the wrap-up you can wait until the end of the summer; just ask your child to make sure there's no food in the backpack. I can't tell you how many times I've come to set up a student at the beginning of the school year only to discover last year's leftover lunch.

Memorabilia for a child.

Memorabilia for the family.

The Elements

The three key elements of the wrap-up will be explored in this chapter:

- Committing to the process
- Making informed decisions
- Storing things properly

COMMITMENT

Making the commitment is sometimes the most challenging step. In fact, it may be as difficult for you as it is for your child to set aside the time for something that doesn't seem so urgent. If you don't make the commitment, however, your child is going to miss out on an extremely important lesson. As with many other organizational skills, the project wrap-up is not taught in school. Whether it's the end of a unit or the end of the year, the last piece of the puzzle is not part of the curriculum. Since there is barely enough time in the classroom to cover required material, sorting and storing old projects is something that needs to be dealt with at home. The sooner you can teach your child these skills, the more space you will have in your home and the easier it will be for your child to live her own life unencumbered by things she no longer uses.

While I don't usually endorse bribing children, I do find that offering the appropriate incentive sometimes gives a kid the push she needs to get started on a project she's dread-

THINK ABOUT IT

You may think it would be easier to do this job *for* your child instead of *with* her. While it might be less of a hassle now, in the long run you'll both lose out. If you don't include your child in the process, you can't impart any skills to her or teach her how to handle projects on her own, which is the true goal of every organizing lesson.

ing. You may suggest that the whole family commit to an end-of-year wrap-up and upon completion do a little show-and-tell with some of the treasures you've dug up. Or you can plan to go out for dinner when the job is done and let your child choose the restaurant. You can also reward her with a movie night with one of her friends or something else you know she will enjoy. Just keep the focus on an activity as opposed to a gift that will turn into more stuff she'll have to find room to store.

MAKING INFORMED DECISIONS

As you clear out your child's backpack and desk you will be teaching her how to distinguish between what's worth keeping and what isn't. While the process is subjective and it's important to respect your child's decisions, you should also help her avoid the "I'll just keep everything" syndrome. The ability to prioritize and assign value to things lies at the core of organization. With this skill, your child will be ahead of the game in school, at home, and in life.

There are some children who instinctively know how to make these decisions and will be able to get through the wrap-up fairly easily. Most students, however, will resist the task completely and thereby fall into one of two categories: *keepers* and *tossers*. As you can imagine, the keepers like to keep everything and the tossers like to toss everything. While they may appear to be polar opposites, they're actually quite similar; neither of them want to bother looking at anything. They don't want to take the time or aren't equipped to decide whether something is worth keeping. Your job is to guide your child and to encourage her to think about what she may want to keep and why. Depending on her temperament and approach, these guidelines will help her handle the paper she's accumulated over the year.

IF YOUR CHILD IS A *KEEPER* BECAUSE:

- **She thinks she will refer to her notes next year:** it's unlikely that your child will look at last year's class notes once the new school year begins, although you will probably not be able to convince her of this. Subjects that build on prior knowledge generally start with a review of the previous year's material (if it's relevant) and then move forward at such a rapid pace that there is no time to look back at old notes. Some children, however, need the comfort of knowing they have old class notes to fall back on. If your child insists that she will use her old notes that's okay. Follow her lead; whatever makes her comfortable should work for you. The process of purging takes time. In three to six months bring the notes out again and let your child figure out if she needed to keep them at all. It's important that she discover for herself whether they were worth keeping; only then will she be able to let things go without fear.

- **She thinks a friend or sibling will want her notes in the future:** again, it's not likely that anyone will look at these notes, but they can be organized and stored outside of your child's room. Take responsibility for storing them yourself; your child's space should be used for things she needs and uses on a regular basis.

- **She doesn't want to look through her papers and deal with the wrap-up:** this is not okay. The two of you need to go through the piles together so you can begin the teaching process. The more she practices purging, the better she will get at it and the easier it will become.

IF YOUR CHILD IS A *TOSSER* BECAUSE:

- **She's not attached to her schoolwork and knows she won't look at it again:** that's fine. If you feel she may regret not having kept anything to look back on in the future, you can practice some "behind the scenes parenting." When you've finished the wrap-up and your child has moved on, pull out one or two items you think she may treasure someday and hold on to them for her. While I normally don't recommend going behind your child's back, in this case she will lose everything unless you salvage it. It takes time for tossers to learn to hold on to things, and you may want to preserve some memories for her until she learns to do it for herself.

- **She had a rough year and doesn't want to have anything left as a reminder:** whether she hated a teacher, did poorly academically, had a tough year socially, or lived through a difficult situation at home, your child may want to get rid of anything associated with the school year. That's okay. Respect her choices and let her learn to trust her instincts.

- **She doesn't want to look through her papers and deal with the wrap-up:** again, not okay. Work through it together even if you have to schedule breaks throughout the process. It shouldn't take long, and it's a skill she needs to learn.

STORING THINGS PROPERLY

While this chapter focuses on short-term storage rather than on long-term archiving, proper storage is still important.

THINK ABOUT IT

It's great to remember that you got 105 percent on a test, but it's not much fun to look back at a page filled with multiple-choice answers or fill-in-the-blank questions. Help your child look for things she'll treasure in the future. Some papers and projects are valuable to a student because of the teacher's comments or because it was her first successful grade in a challenging class. Creative writing, interesting term papers, projects and reports, even tests filled with inspired uses of vocabulary words are often fun to look at years later. You and your child should choose the items you like to read and the ones that make you laugh.

Below you will find general guidelines for storing the papers and projects your child chooses to hold on to at the end of the year.

- **Use archival materials** whenever possible, including boxes, albums, envelopes, and storage bins. While there are no official standards for "archival quality," most products labeled "archival" or "acid-free" are fine for short-term storage. If you want to store something long-term, find out from the manufacturer whether its products are safe for the specific items you want to preserve.
- **Paper** should be stored in acid-free files or folders or in archival poly envelopes. Remove paperclips, rubber bands, and tape from papers before storing them.
- **Separate** highly acidic paper, like newspaper clippings, from other papers so that it doesn't damage them. Store the original in a separate file and keep a photocopy of it with the rest of your papers.
- **Store paper** in a dark container or area, like a closet. Paper should be kept out of the light, particularly sunlight, as much as possible.
- **Memorabilia and stored papers** should be kept out of the basement, attic, and garage whenever possible. Temperature fluctuations and humidity in these areas are harmful to paper and other items and may destroy them over time. Consistently cool and dry storage space is ideal.

These guidelines will help you get old papers and school year paraphernalia out of the way, which is enough of an

accomplishment for most people. If, however, you are interested in preserving your child's papers and memorabilia for
posterity, please refer to the resources listed in the back of
the book for instructions on how to care for the items you
wish to save. There are many archival products on the market
today, as well as many books and Web sites that explain how
to store everything from paper and photographs to books,
textiles, and art.

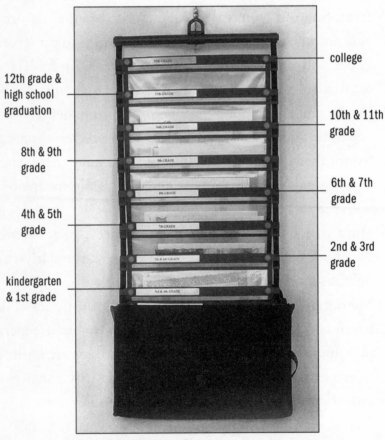

Hanging storage file.

Assessment Questions

These questions will help you create a game plan for the end-of-the-year wrap-up. Once you have a sense of your child's attitude to sorting and purging, and a sense of your own philosophy, you can decide how to approach this phase of the process.

To help determine how your child will approach the end-of-the-year wrap-up

- *What does your child do when she finishes a project?*
  a. She cleans everything up and puts it back where it belongs.
  b. She leaves everything all over the table (or floor or bed).
  c. She doesn't finish projects—she usually finds something more interesting to do about halfway through.

- *What does your child do on the last day of school?*
  a. She dumps her backpack on the floor and leaves it there until September.
  b. She dumps the contents of her backpack on the floor so she can use her backpack over the summer.
  c. She stores everything in a drawer.
  d. She throws everything out.
  e. She leaves her whole backpack at school on the last day of the semester and needs a new one the next year.

- *This school year was:*
  - a. Successful, both academically and personally
  - b. Challenging academically in a particular subject
  - c. Challenging academically in several or all subjects
  - d. Difficult personally (issues at home, at school, or with friends)

- *Your child:*
  - a. Is a keeper
  - b. Is a tosser
  - c. Will take the time to look through her belongings and make decisions

To help you understand your own approach to sorting and saving

- *What have you held on to from your past?*
  - a. A few special mementos
  - b. Boxes of papers and memorabilia
  - c. Nothing; I wish I had some things to look back on.
  - d. Nothing; it doesn't interest me.
  - e. Everything; I can't throw anything out.
  - f. Everything I had was lost (in a fire/flood/hurricane, etc.).

- *Do you enjoy looking at childhood memorabilia?*
  - a. Yes—my scrapbooks/photos/meaningful mementos are well-organized and easily accessible.
  - b. I would love to if I could find anything.

    c. No, it doesn't interest me.

    d. No, nothing was saved or properly preserved.

- *Have you saved anything from your child's early years?*
  a. I have her hospital bracelet, first outfit, baby blanket, and favorite stuffed animal preserved in an archival box.
  b. Everything is still somewhere in her room.
  c. I gave or threw everything away.

- *When you complete a project you:*
  a. Clean everything up and put it back where it belongs
  b. Create clearly labeled files or boxes so you can access the information again in the future
  c. Leave everything all over the table (or floor or bed)
  d. Usually find something more interesting or urgent to do before you can finish a project

- *Are you:*
  a. A keeper
  b. A tosser
  c. Willing to take the time to make decisions

To help determine your and your child's availability and to schedule the wrap-up:

- *What are your child's summer plans?*
  a. She will be home all summer.
  b. She's leaving for the summer immediately after school ends.

c. She's leaving for the summer a few days after school ends.

d. She will be home _____ days/weeks before school starts.

- *When are you available to work with your child? (Specify days and times if your answer is not A.)*
    a. Any day, any time
    b. Weekdays
    c. Weeknights
    d. Weekend days
    e. Weekend evenings

- *What type of schedule works better for you and your child?*
    a. A large block of time on a single day
    b. Small blocks of time spread out over several days

- *What's your deadline for getting this job done?*

To help determine where you will store what your child plans to keep

- *What storage space do you have available? (Be specific in terms of location and amount of actual space available.)*
    a. Closet(s)
    b. Basement
    c. Attic
    d. Garage
    e. File cabinets

f. Drawers

g. Other:_____

Action: Academic Wrap-Up

GATHER SUPPLIES

- Your child should pull together everything she worked on over the course of the year, along with her storage systems, including:
  - The backpack
  - The desktop file box
  - Whatever came home from the locker
  - Any additional loose papers and projects floating around the house and in desk drawers
- Two garbage bags (one for garbage and one for recycling)
- A clear poly envelope, letter or legal size (use the legal size if you need to store oversized projects)
- A permanent marker or label maker
- A camera, if your child has any large or three-dimensional projects

HOW LONG WILL THIS TAKE?

It depends on how much your child has accumulated over the year, but if she's been maintaining her organizational systems, it shouldn't be overwhelming. Plan to work together on this for an hour and a half. If you don't finish, meet again within a couple of days to complete the job.

SORT

Your child will have different types of paper in several different places. Whether she worked in a spiral notebook or in a three-ring binder, she will probably have a couple of hundred pages of notes and a few hundred additional loose sheets of paper in the form of handouts, tests, quizzes, and returned assignments. The first thing she needs to do is *gather all of her paper in one place* so that she can address one subject at a

THINK ABOUT IT

A student can easily end the school year with a thousand pieces of paper. If your child keeps all of it she's not treasuring memories, she's collecting stuff, and if she's going to keep everything every year you're going to have to rent storage space to house it all.

time. This is the most efficient approach because it allows her to see everything pertaining to a single class, which makes it easier to determine what's worth saving and what's redundant or unimportant. It's also the best way to see multiple drafts of a paper or multiple copies of an assignment. This way she can keep only the final version and throw away the others.

Some kids will weed out papers they don't want and throw them out while they're creating their piles. It's not the worst thing to do, but the whole process takes less time if your child simply makes piles without making decisions and then sorts through each pile from top to bottom. She can approach paper sorting in one of two ways:

1. **Gather all of the papers that pertain to a particular subject,** such as math, from the backpack, file box, desk, and any other storage area. When all of the notes, tests, and quizzes for this subject have been collected, she can sort through them, throwing out what she doesn't need and making a pile of what she plans to keep. When all of the math papers have been sorted, she should repeat the process for her other subjects.

2. **Sort through the papers in one storage space at a time** if your child finds it too distracting to move from the backpack to the file box to the desk, shifting from subject to subject. First, have your child empty out her backpack and sort all of the papers into separate piles, one for each subject. She should then sort through all of the papers in the file box, adding to the established piles. She should continue to sort through one storage area at a time until all papers have been separated by subject. When this is done she can address one pile at a time, deciding what to keep and what to throw out for each subject.

    • **If your child worked in a binder** she can take the papers out, add them to the corresponding subject's pile, and address them as she sorts through each subject.

    • **If she worked in spiral notebooks,** she can tear out anything she wants to keep and throw away the rest of the notebook. If she thinks she will use the notes again, keep the notebook intact and store it someplace accessible but out of the way.

Store

- **Store class notes your child is keeping** in a clear poly envelope or in an archival folder. The poly envelopes expand to a depth of two inches, which is enough room to hold approximately one hundred sheets of paper; one envelope should be more than enough to hold a year's worth of memories.

- **Clearly label the envelope or folder** with your child's name, grade, and school year. Add the name of your child's school if it changes frequently, for example, "Hannah, Springfield Middle School, Sixth Grade, 2005–06." If your child wants to keep a particular subject separate she can clip the notes together with a binder clip or store them in a separate, clearly labeled poly envelope. If you're planning to preserve the papers long-term look for an archival plastic clip.

- **Separate the notes your child may want to refer to in the coming year** from memorabilia. Old school notes should be accessible but not take up valuable space on the desk or in the desktop file

> # THINK ABOUT IT
>
> If your child keeps one hundred pieces of paper every year from kindergarten through twelfth grade, she will have thirteen hundred pages to store somewhere in your house. It's hard to imagine anyone sifting through thirteen hundred sheets of paper for fun much less to find something specific.

box, while memorabilia doesn't need to be accessed frequently and should be stored someplace out of the way.

LARGE AND 3-D PROJECTS

Large and three-dimensional items, like science and art projects, do not stand the test of time well. They take up too much space and they generally don't stay in one piece for long.

- **Photograph the project while it's intact.** When the project starts to lose its pieces or fall apart, you can get rid of it while preserving the memory of what it looked like at its best.
- **Store the photos** in an envelope with other work that's being kept from that year.

Pulling Together Loose Ends

THE DESK

While it's not the main part of the academic wrap-up, the desk should also be reorganized before the new school year begins. You can work on it as soon as you're finished with the backpack and paper if you and your child both have the energy.

- **Pull out items that don't belong in the drawers** or that have crept into the wrong section of the desk.

HOW LONG WILL THIS TAKE?

If you've already organized the desk once there should be systems in place that simply need to be restored. Depending on how out of control it's gotten, it should take between half an hour and an hour to get the desk back into shape.

- **Reorganize collections** that still live in the desk and ask your child what she doesn't use or like anymore.
- **Start a shopping list** as you come across supplies that have been nearly or completely used up. Don't rush out to buy supplies—this is where being organized really pays off! Keep the shopping list on a bulletin board or in your wallet so you can find it easily and shop for supplies in August when everything goes on sale. You'll save money twice, first with the sale prices and then by not coming home with a bag full of supplies your child already has or never uses.

THE PORTABLE OFFICE

Approach this as you would the desk. See what needs to be replaced and add it to your shopping list. Ask your child if there was anything she ran out of frequently or didn't have that she needed and add those items to the list as well.

THE COMPUTER

This won't take long, particularly if your child's files and folders are already organized (see chapter 5). Create a new folder labeled with your child's name, grade, and the dates of the school year that just ended. Drop all of the folders, files, and documents that pertain to the school year into the new folder. This should include folders dedicated to specific subjects (for example, English, social studies) as well as any individual files or documents that have to do with assignments or research done over the course of the year.

Print a hard copy of anything important. If your child argues that she can always retrieve the information off the hard drive, remind her that computers often break down and she may be a few upgrades away from her hard drive the next time she wants to read an old paper. Even if she backs her work up onto a floppy disk, Zip disk, or CD, technology is always racing ahead, and there's a good chance that whatever she's using for backup now may soon be obsolete. Your best bet is to keep printed copies of anything important. These can be stored, together with computer backups, in the school year's envelope or file.

Big-Picture Wrap-up

Once the academic wrap-up is complete you can think about the bigger picture. By the time summer rolls around, your child has gathered a year's worth of clothing, magazines, video games, and hair products. She may or may not want you in her bedroom, and it's important to maintain a respectful relationship, but if you're both up for an overhaul now's a good time to do it. You can address as much or as little as you want.

You may want your child to try on clothes to find out what no longer fits and what she no longer wears, go through books and games to separate what she uses from what she doesn't, and/or sort through and clean up any other part of the room to get rid of what's no longer needed and to get ready for the upcoming school year.

Based on volume and experience you can determine approximately how long the whole job will take, and then, depending on your and your child's temperaments and schedules, decide whether you want to lock yourselves in the room for a full day and get it over with or break the project up into two-hour blocks of time over several days. Use the "Zones" that are described in the next chapter, "The Teenager's Bedroom," to determine which areas you want to address and the order in which you plan to attack them.

Maintaining Focus

Your aim is to start a dialog and teach a skill. You want your child to learn to create closure, ensure that work will be available for future use, and clear space, both mental and physical, for the next thing on her list. You also want her to recognize what she's accomplished over the past year and to see how she's grown. While the wrap-up is one of the easiest steps to skip because you don't immediately see how it impacts your child, if you make the commitment now you will understand its value as soon as the new school year begins.

CHAPTER 11

The Final Frontier: The Teenager's Bedroom

A teenager's bedroom is to a teenager what your home as a whole is to you. It is his haven, his base of operations, a reflection of his personal style. It is the place where he entertains guests, displays collections, grooms himself, and works. Whether your teenager's bedroom policy is open-door or enter-and-die, the bedroom is his territory and he expects to be king of his domain.

The most important thing to a parent about your child's bedroom should be its functionality, not its neatness. If your child does his homework, gets good grades, and makes it to school on time, you can probably leave his room alone (although this does not mean he should be allowed to breed unwanted creatures under his bed or let dirty dishes pile up on his desk). If the condition of your child's room seems to be affecting his academic performance, however, it is your prerogative to intervene. Work with your teenager outside of his bedroom first, focusing on other areas of organization. This shows that your priority is your child's academic performance (as opposed to his fight for independence) and the success you share in these areas will help your child trust you.

The hands-on solutions presented in this chapter will guide you through what is often a contentious subject and help you get results that should satisfy both you and your teenager.

The Bedroom of a Teenage Rebel

One day I received a call from the mother of a teenage girl I'd been working with. "You've had quite an effect on my daughter. Her room's so organized now that she decided to paint it. You'll *never* guess what color!"

I didn't have to think twice. "Black." Not only had Nora painted the walls of her room, but she had painted the floor and the ceiling as well. After a pause we both burst out laughing. If this was the next stage of her teenage rebellion, it was okay with us. Nora was fifteen when I met her and failing all of her subjects. She was referred to me by her therapist, who was concerned that this bright girl had totally shut down in school. When I arrived for our first appointment Nora was still asleep. After being woken by her mother, she dragged herself out of bed, left her boyfriend asleep in her room, and emerged with a cigarette dangling from her mouth.

A quick mental inventory of Nora's numerous body piercings told me that I had no more than fifteen minutes to win her over. Nora agreed to work with me—*once*. Since I knew I wouldn't be able to hold her attention for long, I crammed two hours of organizing into one and set her up in record time. Nora agreed to see me again.

By our fourth session, Nora was keeping track of her assignments and papers and her grades were picking up. Since I had proven myself with my organizing techniques and had gained Nora's trust, we were able to move to the next stage; she let me into her bedroom. It was a disaster area. The floor was covered with clothes, her desk was littered with CDs and magazines, and there was not an inch of wall visible beneath her collection of heavy metal posters. I followed her lead and together we came up with solutions for the issues she deemed important.

"I need to do my own laundry. How do I do it?" Our first lesson was how to use the washing machine. "I don't want to put my clothes away." Our second lesson was how to live out of two different colored laundry baskets, one for clean clothes and one for dirty. During our next session we organized Nora's desk and the surrounding area so she could find what she needed, and then we were done. The posters were still on the walls and the clothes were still visible, but her room was habitable and she was able to work effectively in her own space.

When Nora's mother told me about her daughter's adventures in decorating neither of us was alarmed. We both knew that Nora was keeping her room neat and organized—who cared what color the walls were? Her mother and I were focused on her schoolwork and organizing abilities instead of on areas that were not part of her academic life. The black paint, the body piercing, the boyfriend—when these hot-button issues were taken out of the equation, and Nora knew

she wasn't being judged or criticized, she was able to concentrate on how to succeed in school. I provided Nora with
the one tool she really needed: the ability to focus on the help
that was being offered instead of fighting about grades or behavior. Nora pursued her studies with a drive she had never
before exhibited. She went from failing all of her courses to
getting straight A's, and graduated half a year early, black
walls and all.

ANALYSIS

■ If the state of your child's room isn't interfering with her academic performance, leave it alone.

■ Separate academic and nonacademic issues. Nora's
mother did an exceptional job of getting her daughter help in
school by leaving other areas of Nora's life out of it. The smok-
ing, the boyfriend, and other manifestations of teenage rebellion were dealt with separately and secondarily—the primary
focus was getting Nora up to speed in school.

When to Intervene

The way children decorate their walls, paint their rooms,
and maintain (or don't maintain) their space is an expres-
sion of an emerging sense of self. Again, as long as it doesn't
interfere with their academic success—or become a health

hazard—I say, let them express themselves. But there *are* times when the state of the bedroom is clearly having a negative impact on a student's academic performance. If your child can't find his assignments, has no room on his desk to do his homework, or is always scrambling to find clean clothes, he's going to have difficulty succeeding in school. Living in a disorganized or dirty room can also be depressing. It can effect a child's outlook and the way he presents himself, which will in turn effect the way he performs in school.

I began working with Mark during his sophomore year. His room was certainly not the neatest I'd ever seen—his floor was buried beneath piles of clothes and the surface of his desk had not been visible for quite some time—but I was focused on academic issues, and we spent the year discussing and organizing his schoolwork. We met sporadically and Mark's progress varied. When I was called in at the end of the school year to help him prepare for final exams, it had been three months since our last appointment. As I surveyed his half-empty binder and partially used planner, Mark looked at me and said, "The truth is, when I use your systems they work. I just don't always want to use them. I don't always care."

Mark's mom had advised me that Mark was seeing a therapist, so I knew there were other issues affecting his attitude towards school and his ability to self-motivate. My job was to help him get organized so that he could take control of his academics as soon as he was ready. I didn't realize how big that job was going to be until that June day, when Mark finally agreed to let me work with him in his bedroom. It was stiflingly hot and I asked if we could turn on the air conditioner. Mark said sure but warned me that it didn't work very well. I climbed over the drum set that was blocking the window and turned on the air conditioner. Mark was right—it wheezed a trickle of lukewarm air into the room that did nothing to relieve the heat. I turned it off and checked the filter. It was so filthy I realized it had probably never been changed.

Before I climbed back over the drum set I ran my fingers along the window blinds. My fingertips came up black; the virtually inaccessible blinds could not have been cleaned in the last year. As I took a closer look at my surroundings I realized that the sheets on the bed were dirty and were probably not being changed frequently, and the soda cans and dirty food plates all over the room would soon be attracting unwanted visitors. The room had moved beyond teenage slovenliness and entered the realm of health hazard.

I called Mark's mom that night. I told her that as a rule I don't care what a kid's room looks like, but in this case I felt the condition of Mark's bedroom was interfering with his academic performance and possibly with his health, both physical and mental. She was shocked. Mark's parents were both busy professionals and they had full-time household help, but they believed, as many parents do, that their child's room was his own responsibility, and they didn't want anyone else cleaning it for him. This may be a good philosophy, but it doesn't work unless parents' expectations are reasonable and explained clearly to the child. There's also a difference between picking up after oneself and heavy-duty cleaning. Your child may be expected to do both, but he has to know that it's expected of him and he has to know how to do it.

In Mark's case it became clear that he was expected to make his bed, put his clothes away, clear out dirty dishes, and make sure all areas of the room were easily accessible. He would get help with regular and heavy cleaning, like laundry, cleaning the blinds, and changing the air conditioner filter. The dust bunnies and collections that were growing under the bed were banished. Mark's mom immediately replaced his sheets, moved the heavy furniture, and worked on cleaning out a year's worth of dirt. In the meantime, Mark and I went through drawers and cabinets, sorting and purging their contents. Mark's mom laid the groundwork for the future by helping Mark with the things he couldn't do on his own and by teaching him how to maintain a clean room by himself. By the following September Mark was in a better place, both physically and emotionally, and he excelled during his junior year.

One important thing to note here is that if it hadn't been the right time for Mark, we wouldn't have been successful in changing his room. His mom and I might have been able to force the issue, but he wouldn't have followed through on his own, and it wouldn't have resulted in a positive impact on his academics. When we finally addressed his room Mark was emotionally prepared to make changes; he was ready to be proud of his environment and to accept responsibility for maintaining it. Just as he knew my systems worked for school even though he didn't always want to use them, he saw that they could work at home too when he was willing to put them into practice.

ANALYSIS

■ You need to distinguish between messy and neglected. You may not mind the fact that your child chooses his wardrobe off the floor, but he shouldn't be sleeping on dirty sheets or playing host to a colony of ants.

■ Determine what you expect from your child, explain it to him, and then show him how to do it. The information and the skills have to come from you before he can maintain systems on his own.

■ Timing is everything. It took Mark a year before he was able to accept responsibility for his room and for his schoolwork; if your child isn't ready, don't push him. You can reintroduce the concept in new ways at other times. What doesn't work today may work tomorrow.

Breaking It Down

If you have a hard time keeping things organized around your home, you may be concerned that you don't have the skills to help your child. Don't worry. There is a system for sorting through and setting up a kid's bedroom, and you will be able to follow it, step by step, whether or not you have faith in your own organizing skills.

Every household is run differently. However cleaning duties are assigned in your home, you can establish ground rules and break down chores as explicitly as possible. Remember that your child can't read your mind—something may be obvious to you, but it may not be at all clear to him. When you say, "Clean up your room," do you mean, "make your bed," "vacuum," "do your laundry," or "change the air conditioner filter?" Show and tell: do the job together, explain what you are asking your child to do, and show him how to do it.

When my kids were growing up I gave them the leeway to live their lives within certain parameters. What went on in their bedrooms (up to a certain point) was their business. But I also gave them the skills they needed to maintain a basic level of organized living. I tried to make sure my kids always knew how to do what I asked them to do, and I made it easy for them to be successful at their tasks. When they reached a certain age, for example, my sons were responsible for making their own beds. This was tricky, since they shared a bunk bed, and it's not easy to straighten out sheets on a bed that's up against a wall, particularly one that's five feet off the ground. My solution was to cover the mattresses with fitted sheets, and use comforters in duvet covers instead of flat sheets. The covers could be laundered separately (instead of sheets) and the kids had one less thing to worry about.

I wanted to offer my kids a solution that would lead to continued success. In this case it was easy. The bed was made when the blanket was folded and placed at the foot of the bed. Were the blankets folded as neatly as I could have folded them? Of course not. But this approach was at least within the realm of possibility for my kids. The boys were happy because the whole process took less than a minute, and I was happy because their beds looked neat. Think about what you expect from your child and from his room, and then consider how he can achieve it easily. And remember, it's never too late—you can start teaching this skill at any age.

While I have been organizing children professionally for many years, I don't want to give you the false (and unrealistic) impression that my teenagers' bedrooms were easily and peacefully maintained all the time. My kids may have made their beds on a fairly regular basis, but the best trick I learned for staying happy with their rooms was to close the bedroom door. I also accepted that my children's rooms were not necessarily a reflection of me. I had an entire home in which to express my sense of style and personality and that is what my guests saw, not the shrines to baseball players or the stacks of clean laundry that never made it back into the drawers. I didn't care what my kids' rooms looked like because no one had to see them. Still, there were times when I did clear out their bedrooms, either with or without them. I knew, however, that I was doing this to satisfy my own needs. If it's important to you to keep a meticulous house, and you can't bring yourself to simply close the door on your teenager's bedroom, then you have to acknowledge that you're cleaning for yourself and not for your child.

While I mostly let my boys do what they wanted in their rooms, I did have a different set of rules for the spaces we shared. Common areas such as the kitchen or living room were expected to be kept neat and clear of personal clutter. No one was allowed to dump his coat on the hall floor. Dirty shoes were left outside and muddy or wet clothes were taken off in the bathroom. Football clothes were tossed directly into the bathtub and rinsed before going in the laundry. Everyone had to put his dirty dishes in the sink or dishwasher. If someone was working at the kitchen table, he had to clean up all of his papers and supplies when he was finished (or before dinner, whichever came first). Tell your child that you respect what he does in his own room and that you expect him to respect the guidelines you've set up for the rest of your home.

Springing for the Taxidermist

Several years ago my family and I were visiting my parents in Florida. It was an emotionally difficult time because my parents weren't well, and my husband decided to cheer our sons up by taking them on a deep-sea fishing expedition. The boys were thrilled when they each caught a fish, and in a brief moment of insanity my husband agreed to have the fish sent to a taxidermist. A few months later two huge boxes arrived on my doorstep. Inside were two stuffed fish and a $500 invoice. I was in shock. Not only was $500 an outrageous sum of money to spend on stuffed *anything*, I now had two huge, glassy-eyed fish that needed to be incorporated into my urban chic decorating scheme. There was not much I could do about it, so I hung the fish up in the boys' rooms. Needless to say, they did not last long, well-preserved as they were. My sons

managed to destroy $500 worth of stuffed fish within a few
weeks with a couple of games of indoor basketball, and I
learned never to invest too much money in a teenager's bedroom.

Fishing expedition.

ANALYSIS

■ We all do things in moments of weakness, or in an effort to try to make up for things that aren't going well. It's normal. Don't harp on it—move on.

■ Kids can destroy anything. I suggest keeping expensive or otherwise valuable items out of your kid's room in order to avoid the pain, frustration, and expense of replacing things that get destroyed in the course of a teenager's everyday life.

■ Try to avoid using glass ceiling fixtures or globes or lamps with glass or ceramic bottoms in your child's room—all it takes is one indoor football game to demolish a glass fixture and to end up with a potentially dangerous situation.

Assessment Questions

Use these questions to gather as much information as possible about your child's living conditions and habits in order to determine your priorities. The questions will also lead you to examine your own expectations for this process and for your child. When you have completed the questions you can create a plan with your child for reorganizing and maintaining his bedroom.

To identify the big picture of the bedroom

- *Does it seem like the state of your child's bedroom is interfering with his performance in school?*

- *Does your child share a room?*
  - If so, are the room's occupants compatible in their style and habits? If they aren't:
    - Separate the space, if you can, to give each child a sense of privacy or autonomy; consider using a screen or a bookcase to divide the room.
    - Work with each child separately to meet his needs and sense of style.
    - If one child has an earlier bedtime, it will be difficult for the other child to do homework in the bedroom. Designate another area in your home as his workspace.

- *What is the overall feeling you get from walking into your child's room?*
  - a. Calm, serene, peaceful
  - b. Chaotic and overwhelming
  - c. Messy but tolerable
  - d. You couldn't live in it, but your child seems to be doing fine.
  - e. There's not enough floor space to walk into the room.
  - f. It's too distressing—you try not to go in at all.

- *Can you identify separate areas in the room being used for different functions (working, sleeping, grooming, entertaining, and collecting)?*

- *Is your child's space clear or cluttered?*
  - a. There is a place for everything and everything is in its place.
  - b. There is a place for nothing and everything is all over the place.

c. Clutter mainly comes from papers and books

d. Clutter mainly comes from clothes

e. Clutter mainly comes from hobbies (musical instruments, art supplies, comic books)

f. Clutter includes grooming supplies, jewelry, and accessories, CDs, and candy wrappers

To assess your child's storage needs and options

- *Are there more items than there is space to store them?*

- *What kind of storage space is available?*
  a. Bookshelves
  b. Closet
  c. Under the bed
  d. Desk drawers
  e. Dresser
  f. Cabinet
  g. Outside of the bedroom
  h. Other: _____

- *Is the available storage space being used efficiently right now?*

- *Can you identify specific areas of trouble?*
  a. The desk
  b. The floor
  c. The bed
  d. Under the bed

e. The closet

f. The dresser

g. The bookshelves

h. All of the above

To help clarify both your own expectations and those of your child

- *How do you expect your child's room to look?*
  a. Immaculate
  b. The bed should be made and the surfaces should be clear.
  c. It can be messy during the week but should be cleaned up on the weekend.
  d. It doesn't matter—I never go in there.

- *What do you expect your child to be responsible for in his room?*
  a. He should keep the room neat (put away clean laundry, make his bed).
  b. He should keep the room clean (do the laundry himself, vacuum).
  c. He should keep the room *really* clean (wash the windows, change the air conditioner filter).
  d. He should be able to find his homework quickly and clean clothes easily, even if that means working out of laundry baskets or piles on the floor.
  e. I don't expect him to do anything—someone else will do it for him.

- *What does it mean to your child when you ask him to clean his room?*

- *How many changes do you expect to make?*
    a. None
    b. Some (list specific areas)
    c. I plan to do a complete overhaul

- *Do you plan to include your child in the process and if so, how?*

- *Ask your child to describe his dream room. If he could make five changes (within parameters, such as within a certain budget), what would they be? This is an important step no matter how old your child is; make the parameters clear, say you'll do your best to accommodate his wishes, and then let him make his own decisions.*
    - Sample changes: exchange a twin bed for a double, get a sofa or beanbag chair, have a TV in his room, get new sheets, paint the room, have more space for his books

HOW LONG WILL THIS TAKE?

This depends on the state of the room, your child, and how much you plan to tackle. It can take anywhere from a few hours to several months. Decide with your child whether you prefer marathon sessions on the weekend or two-hour sessions whenever you both have time. Stick to the time limit, and always leave yourself at least twenty minutes to clean up before each session is over.

Action: Organizing Your Child's Bedroom

Use the Assessment Questions and conversations with your child to decide what changes you are going to make. Will you be mainly purging and reorganizing or adding storage space and new supplies? Will you be moving furniture or completely redecorating? Decide on your budget and consult your child about his wish list. Determine how much your child will be involved in the process and set a specific time to start.

Keep in mind (and inform your child) that it always gets worse before it gets better. You will be pulling the bedroom apart, and it's probably going to get ugly. Focus on one area at a time and see it through to the end. One small success will be the encouragement you and your child need to continue.

STEP ONE: PURGE

- **Come armed** with garbage bags and cleaning supplies.
- **Identify the zones in your child's room.** A teenager's bedroom is generally broken down into zones in which five main functions take place:
  - Working
  - Sleeping
  - Grooming
  - Entertaining
  - Collecting

You can create a map of the room delineating each area and estimate how long it will take to address.

- **Once you identify the zones, start purging.** Most people hate this part the most, but it has to be done. Guide your child through the process but let him make final decisions about what to keep and what to toss. You can always revisit the area again in a few months.

- **Establish some basic guidelines for purging before you begin.** For example, decide that you will get rid of games that are broken or missing pieces; makeup or hair products that have changed color, consistency, or scent; and books your child doesn't think he'll read again.

> ## THINK ABOUT IT
>
> Keep in mind that the less stuff there is, the more surface area is clear and the easier the room will be for your child to maintain.

- **Set up a box or bag for items in good condition that you plan to donate.** It's always easier to part with something when you know someone else will enjoy it.

- **Keep the focus on a single area.** This can be emotionally draining and exhausting work, so don't bite off more than you can chew.

- **Do not leave the room.** When you come across items that don't belong in your child's bedroom just pile them outside the door. You can return them to their proper places when you're finished in the bedroom; leaving the room while you're working will take you off track, and the bedroom will take three times longer to complete.

- **Go through the process in small increments:** clothing one day; papers another; books, music, cosmetics another. Group together categories that take less time.

- **Clean each area thoroughly** after you purge its contents before you put anything back.

STEP TWO: ORGANIZE

Once you're finished purging you can see how much empty storage space you actually have. You can then organize one area at a time, focusing on the specific function of each particular zone. You may need to bring in new supplies (magazine holders, extra shelving, storage for clothes) and come up with alternative solutions for items that take up too much space (storage for out-of-season clothing or sports equipment, perhaps outside of the bedroom).

When you're considering storage options, don't forget the walls! If you're short on space, walls can provide an excellent opportunity to create storage where there was none. Bookshelves, wall shelving, cubbies, and hooks can be used to increase storage without taking up much, if any, floor space.

THINK ABOUT IT

As you redesign your child's bedroom, keep in mind the following questions:

■ Have we made it easy to maintain this bedroom?

■ Are the systems user-friendly?

■ Does everything have a home?

■ Can everything be accessed easily?

WORK ZONE

If you haven't completed the desk setup already, it's a good place to start. It places the priority on your child's academics rather than on other aspects of his life.

If your child doesn't have a desk in his room, make sure he has a portable office and/or a designated workspace outside of the bedroom. Set up a small work zone in his room where he can store his portable office, backpack, and other school-related items when they're not being used. See Chapter 6, "The Desk and the Portable Office," for guidelines.

SLEEP ZONE

This zone includes your child's bed and the surrounding area. If you expect him to make his bed, make sure he knows how to make it and simplify the process as much as possible.

Decide with your child what he needs near his bed and then assign each item a permanent and convenient spot on a night table or nearby shelf. To minimize the clutter encourage your child to think about what he actually uses when he's in bed. The list may include some of the following items:

- Alarm clock
- Lamp
- Eyeglasses
- Water
- Tissues

- One or two books or magazines
- Journal
- Pen and paper
- Lip balm, hand lotion

GROOMING ZONE

While many kids have room to store their shampoo, hair gel, and makeup in the bathroom, much grooming still takes place in the bedroom. Bottles and brushes and tubes and vials tend to find their way into every corner of the room, making it more time-consuming to get ready in the morning than it has to be.

Designate a grooming zone for your child. Find out where he usually does his preparations and think about what needs to be changed in order to make it a more efficient workspace. Accommodate his habits instead of trying to force him to change them. Any clear surface will work, from the top of a dresser to a shelf in a closet, as long as it's near a mirror and an electrical outlet. If surface space is limited, your child can assemble a portable grooming zone in a basket or caddy. Create a storage spot for the supplies when they're not being used.

IF YOUR CHILD GROOMS:

- **At his dresser,** use the dresser surface.

- **At his desk, on his bed, or at a standing mirror,** use a caddy that he can stow away when he's finished.

THINK ABOUT IT

Always keep a trash can near the grooming zone. Make it easy for your child to get rid of used tissues, cotton balls, empty bottles, and old products, and the grooming zone will require less maintenance. If there's no room for a standard trash basket, use a mini–trash can designed for desktops.

Multiple trash cans in the bedroom are even better. How many kids do you know who will walk across the room to throw away a piece of garbage? And even if your child is a great shot, trash-can basketball usually results in wads of paper, soda cans, and banana peels sitting on the floor for days.

- **At a mirror on his closet door,** use a caddy that can be kept on a closet shelf or store his supplies in clear plastic shoe pockets that can hang over the closet door.

ASSEMBLE THE GROOMING ZONE

- **Have your child make a list of** supplies he uses on a regular basis (i.e., hairbrush, deodorant, cotton balls) so that you know how much storage space he will need. Figure out whether the supplies will fill a small plastic caddy, two baskets, or an entire drawer.
- **Gather all of the supplies** and store them appropriately in the grooming zone:
  - Place anything that can get wet or sticky (like bottles of hair spray or perfume) on a tray so they don't leave rings on the furniture.

- Gather like items in separate containers. Brushes and combs can be held upright in one jar; cotton balls can be stored in another.
- If your child has a lot of makeup or hair accessories, she can use a small set of plastic drawers to hold everything. She should sort the items by category and assign each category a drawer. She can label each drawer if she wants to. Alternatively, she can use several small bowls or containers to hold the different types of makeup and accessories. The key is to keep each category separate so that she can easily find and return what she uses.

ENTERTAINING ZONE

Even if you have a large home, it's likely that your teenager migrates to his bedroom when his friends come over. What they do when they hang out there defines the entertaining zone. If they play video games they need someplace to sit within reach of the television or computer; if they are forming a band they need someplace to play within reach of electrical outlets. My experience, through years of bedroom makeovers, has been that teenagers want to make the room user-friendly for their friends, and what they want most is a sofa. This zone will be defined by how much space is available and what you're willing to tolerate. Just make sure you're clear about the rules.

Establish guidelines and discuss them with your child. Let him know that it is his responsibility to make sure they are followed, and make him aware of the consequences for ignoring the rules. Then hand over control. Here are a few sample topics you may want to establish an understanding about:

- **Open/Closed-Door Policy.** This can vary, depending on the situation and on your family's attitude towards privacy.
- **Food in the bedroom.** Some ground rules may include:
  - All dirty dishes and food-related trash needs to be out of the room before bedtime.
  - Drinks are allowed in the room but not food.
  - None of your child's guests can leave the house until all food and drinks are cleared out of the bedroom. Your child can then rally his friends into helping him clean his room or take responsibility for everything himself.
  - No food or drinks allowed in the room—ever.
- **Wet towels.** They tend to live on bedroom floors. I rarely come across a teen who will take his wet towel back to the bathroom; to counter this, try attaching a hook to the back of your child's bedroom door so he can hang his towels up in his bedroom.

COLLECTING ZONE

Children are collectors. From stuffed animals to baseball cards, jewelry to CDs, the collections grow and change as your child does. Collections are generally housed in the bedroom, but we rarely account for them when designing a child's room. Space needs to be designated for displaying and storing your child's collections, and old collections need to be cleared away to make room for new ones.

Abandoned collections may be thrown out, pared down, or archived. This is an excellent opportunity for your child to learn how to manage and properly store collections that are important to him and to part with those that aren't in order to make space for the new things in his life.

- Before you can designate an area for a specific collection you need to know how much space it will take up. Will it fit on a shelf? Does it need an entire bookcase? To estimate the volume of a collection, you must first identify all of its parts and gather them all together.
- Clear enough space on the floor, bed, or desk to sort your child's collections and then create separate piles for each one.
- Ask your child which collections are current, which he'd like to keep but doesn't need access to on a regular basis, and which he is ready to get rid of.
- If someone else might want any of the collections he's ready to part with, put them in bags or boxes and move them out of the bedroom. Donate, sell, or give them away as soon as possible. If they're not worth saving, throw them out right away.
- For the old collections he wants to keep, decide what type of storage and how much space they will need (refer to the list below for suggestions).
- Of his current collections, determine which will be displayed and which can be stored. Find out how frequently he wants to access the stored collections before assigning them a storage spot.

- Determine how much storage and display space you will need all together, and list the storage supplies (bins, albums, extra shelving) you will need to complete the job.
- Refer to the storage guidelines in chapter 10 when storing or archiving your child's collections. The basic rule to keep in mind is that if something is precious to your child you should treat it like a relative (a relative you *like*)— keep it dry and close; don't store it in the basement, attic, or garage.

Storage Options for Things that Live in Your Child's Room

- **Art**
  - **Art supplies:** art supply bin or tackle box; set of standing drawers (plastic or metal); clear plastic bins, labeled according to contents
  - **Art books:** shelf space
  - **Camera and film:** camera case
  - **Posters and prints:** frames, wall space, cardboard tubes, plastic poster protectors
- **Card collections:** three-ring binders with plastic inserts for cards; plastic bins or shoeboxes
- **Games**
  - **Board games, cards:** shelf space, baskets, or bins
  - **Video games:** bin or case for game cartridges, plastic bin for video game console, plastic ties for wires
- **Jewelry:** jewelry box, small decorative boxes, necklace tree, mesh screen to hold earrings

- **Music**
  - **Cassette tapes and CDs:** cassette holder, CD binder, standing or mounted cassette or CD holders
  - **Instruments:** shelf or closet space designated for instrument, instrument case or bag, binder and plastic sleeves or folders for sheet music
- **Photographs**
  - **Loose photographs:** photo albums, cardboard boxes, plastic bins
  - **Negatives or photo CDs:** three-ring binder with plastic sleeves for negatives or CDs, archival negative box
- **Reading material**
  - **Books:** shelf space, cardboard boxes or plastic bins for books being stored
  - **Comic books:** plastic sleeves for individual comics, narrow cardboard boxes designed to hold comic books
  - **Magazines:** magazine rack, fabric or wicker basket
- **Sports equipment**
  - **Bats, racquets, lacrosse, or hockey sticks:** tall garbage pail, closet corner
  - **Balls:** mesh or plastic laundry bin, mesh laundry bag
  - **Helmets:** hooks on the wall, back of door, or in the closet
  - **If the sports equipment doesn't fit in your child's room,** create a central area somewhere else in your home to store everything together
- **Stamps, Stickers:** albums
- **Stationery:** shoebox or bin, desk drawer

RULE OF THUMB

When you fill your child's bookshelves aim to cover about two thirds of each shelf. His collections are going to grow and you want him to have enough space to store new additions.

Regular Maintenance

Like other organizational skills maintaining his room will probably be new to your child, and he will need help at first. Be realistic about how much you expect from your teenager. Most teens live busy lives; they get up without a lot of time to spare, rush to school, come home late, and have hours of homework. Consider what would be realistic to ask him to do based on his schedule. Does he have more time to spare on school days or on weekends? Also keep in mind that various times throughout the school year will be more or less pressured and busy. There is no hard-and-fast rule about what you should require of your child, but *if you make his responsibilities realistic for his lifestyle, he can live up to them.*

Once you've established the ground rules (who makes the bed, when the trash gets taken out, where the wet towels go), observe how your child lives in his space. He may make changes right away or adapt his new systems to better fit his needs over time. Don't pester him about keeping his room in perfect condition. Don't expect to do a big cleanup with him every week (unless you want to be denied access to his bed-

room permanently). Plan to help him put his room back together on a monthly basis. Respect his privacy, his schedule,
and his needs, and above all remember that you're doing this
first and foremost to help him succeed in school.

CHAPTER 12

Oh, Yes— Expect the Unexpected

You already possess the tool you will need most as you teach your child how to organize: your intuition. There will be visible cues to direct your attention to the breakdown in your child's academic strategies, but sometimes you will need to use your sixth sense to unearth the issues that lie at the heart of your child's frustration. It can be difficult to fathom what goes on in children's minds. They have wonderful imaginations that sometimes play terrible tricks on them, and it's important to look beyond external signs to find out if there's something else going on. Follow your instincts and keep your eye on what you're really after—the root of the problem and not just the fallout.

This lesson was hammered home for me during one fascinating encounter. I will never forget working with Raymond, a twelve-year-old who had suddenly fallen behind in school. His mother called me, anxious that her son wasn't bringing home his homework or handing anything in. When I arrived at their home I did what I always do first and asked Raymond for permission to empty his backpack; he said no. I was surprised—no one had ever refused my request before. I tried to coax him gently, but he was adamant that we not touch his bag. I was at a bit of a loss; if I couldn't see his books and papers I couldn't know what I was dealing with, so there was not much I could do.

I knew we would have to return to the backpack, but I started with something else in order to make Raymond comfortable and to gain his trust. He seemed perfectly content as we set up a new binder together, but when I suggested that we collect his old papers from the backpack so we could add them to his binder, he panicked. "No, no, no, no, no!" he shouted, and, close to tears, he started to gag.

After some time I was able to calm him down and finally uncover the source of his anxiety. Several weeks before, while reaching into his backpack for his bus pass, Raymond had touched something gooey in his bag; at the same moment he looked down and saw that he was about to step on a crushed dead bird on the street. The two events immediately became associated in his mind and he hadn't opened his backpack since. This explained why Raymond's homework was no longer coming home and why he wasn't equipped for class each day. It wasn't that he was disorganized, it was that he refused to open his bag because he was terrified of what he thought he would find inside it! This strange scenario had a huge impact on his ability to function in school and therefore had a huge impact on his academic performance. I told the traumatized boy to take a break, and I cleaned out his bag with his mother.

This backpack situation was one of the worst I'd ever seen. We didn't know exactly how long it had been since Raymond had put his hand in his backpack, but the gooey mess he had associated with the dead bird was some very old leftover lunch. I also found keys, money, and several other things Raymond had been missing. His mom ran the backpack through the washing machine and by the time I left we had put everything back together.

The most interesting thing I discovered when I went through his backpack was that Raymond had several good organizational systems already set up, and he had been using them consistently until the bird fiasco. Normally I would not have been called in to work with this child. Raymond may have teetered on the brink of disorganization in the past, but the only reason he had completely fallen apart now was because he had seen a dead bird on the street.

Children live in their own worlds of fantasies and fears. When they experience traumatic events, they tend to turn inward, as Raymond did. He had been unable to tell his mother what had happened; all she saw was his downward spiral in school. She assumed it was an academic/organizational issue and called me in to help, but I ended up playing the role of a detective more than anything else. When I learned what Raymond was hiding I understood why he'd stopped functioning in school. Raymond never needed a major overhaul—a single incident had triggered a breakdown, and once we resolved it I didn't need to work with Raymond again. After a few follow-up phone calls I knew Raymond was back on track and would be fine on his own.

Out of Order

Sometimes the clue to why something doesn't work for your child will be more obvious. Thirteen-year-old Katie had weak visual-spatial skills. This weakness clearly manifested itself in her bedroom, which was always a mess. Shoes and clothes were abandoned wherever they were removed, plastic wrappers from new CDs littered the floor, and papers that were no longer needed were left on the desk to pile up. Katie's physical disorganization had always been more of an annoyance than an impediment; she was a brilliant student and had been able to maintain an A average, relying on excellent cerebral organizational skills to get her through school. The demands of junior high, however, were now straining her intellectual resources, and her lack of physical organizational skills was becoming increasingly problematic. More classes and a heavier workload made it difficult to keep track of deadlines and other obligations in her head, and she was starting to feel the strain.

Katie was unprepared for tests because she forgot they were coming up; she was unable to complete her homework because she often left her textbooks in school; and when she did complete assignments she often left them home. As we set up new organizational systems I could see the added difficulties Katie experienced as a result of her weak visual-spatial perception. In particular, when we assembled her binder I recognized that sequence and color were unimportant to her, although I didn't realize how little they meant until she called me, confused, halfway through the year.

"My binder fell off my chair in school and everything sort of exploded. I tried to put it back together, but it doesn't look the same."

When we met and I saw the binder I understood why— the subjects were completely out of order. Katie had managed to get all of her papers back in the binder, but it never occurred to her that the subjects had been arranged in a specific sequence and that the sequence could be easily reassembled by following the order of the divider tabs. She didn't see the order, she didn't see that the tabs were staggered, *she didn't see any pattern at all.*

We took everything out of the binder, and I talked Katie through the process of reassembling it from scratch. "I want you to notice that there are several different colors. Each subject has its own color; maybe you can remember the order of the colors. The yellow divider comes first because the tab is at the very top. The blue divider comes next because its tab fits right under the yellow tab. If you look at all of the tabs together you see that they make a fan. Each section is a part of the fan and they go in order, from top to bottom." By using language instead of relying on her visual skills Katie was able to discern a pattern and talk herself through the process on her own.

When you're working with your child you may stumble across roadblocks she trips over all the time. The brain is a fascinating instrument; I will never cease to be amazed by the hurdles it sets up for people to jump over. But the same brain that comes up with the problems can also come up with some ingenious solutions. Once you figure out what's getting in your child's way you can figure out how to help her overcome it, whether it means going over, under, or around the wall.

Long-term Investment

Organizing your child is a long-term investment. The process requires both commitment and patience, and the effects of your hard work aren't always apparent right away. Don't lose heart if you feel like your child isn't absorbing everything you say. She may take to one tool quickly and not be able to focus on the others yet; she may not be ready to hear anything at all. Just because you don't see an immediate and complete turnaround, it doesn't mean that you've wasted your time. Everything you do registers in some part of your child's brain. When she's ready to use the information it will be there.

I've worked with students who sit passively through a session, and when I see them next it's obvious they've abandoned their systems. Time after time we set up the tools and time after time they don't get used, but I don't give up and I don't judge them. I'm always happily surprised on the day, perhaps the next semester, perhaps two years down the road, when I walk in and see that the lightbulb's gone off. Suddenly the student is ready to go; she's paying attention, asking questions, implementing systems without my having to explain them. Many kids even call me to make the appointment themselves when they know they're ready. Your child has to be in the right frame of mind to act on what you've taught her. If she's not ready now, she will be someday, and you will have laid the groundwork.

My son Noah used to delight in taunting me, as only a teenager could, by pointing out my glaring inadequacy. "Hey, Mom," he would snicker, "how come you can help everybody else get organized but you can't help me? You've given people advice on national television and your own son still starts papers the night before they're due!" I tried to help him, I truly did, but my firstborn wasn't interested. And then he left for college and I wondered if I had managed to fail him in the one area where I should have been best equipped to help him.

Noah had been at school for six weeks when my phone rang. It turned out that I had not, in fact, ruined his life. "Mom," he reflected, with all the wisdom of a college freshman, "I know I'm not the smartest kid here. But I really think I'm the most organized." My heart skipped a beat. He continued, "Nobody here has time management skills, no one has filing systems, and no one really knows how to tackle a long-term assignment."

Bells were ringing, angels were singing—I had done it! I had invested these skills in my son, and he was blossoming before my eyes. I couldn't believe that Noah had, at long last, recognized the value of what I had taught him; I was nearly blushing at the thought of being thanked by my son.

Noah went on, full of amazement and gratitude, "Wasn't my high school wonderful?"

My jaw dropped. Was he kidding?! *His high school?!*

Did he not remember how hard I'd worked to help him succeed as I knew he could? How I'd believed in him and supported him and encouraged him, sometimes into the wee hours of the morning? And then I realized it didn't matter. What difference did it make who got the credit—the job was done. I smiled, laughed to myself, and answered, "Honey, they were the best."

FURTHER READING

Housekeeping

Ager, Stanley, and Fiona St. Aubyn. *Ager's Way to Easy Elegance*. New York: Bobbs-Merrill Company, Inc., 1980.

Mendelson, Cheryl. *Home Comforts: The Art & Science of Keeping House*. New York: Scribner, 1999.

Pinkham, Mary Ellen. *Mary Ellen's Clean House!: The All-in-One-Place Encyclopedia of Contemporary Housekeeping*. New York: Crown Publishers, Inc., 1993.

Learning Differences

Dawson, Peg, and Richard Guare. *Executive Skills in Children and Adolescents*. New York: The Guilford Press, 2004.

Hallowell, Edward M., and John J. Ratey. *Answers to Distraction*. New York: Bantam Books, 1994.

―――. *Driven to Distraction: Recognizing and Coping with Attention Deficit Disorder from Childhood Through Adulthood.* New York: Touchstone, 1994.

Hartmann, Tom. *ADD: Simple Exercises That Will Change Your Daily Life.* Grass Valley, CA: Underwood Books, 1998.

Kolberg, Judith, and Kathleen Nadeau. *ADD-Friendly Ways to Organize Your Life.* New York: Brunner-Routledge, 2002.

Levine, Mel. *All Kinds of Minds: A Young Student's Book About Learning Abilities and Learning Disorders.* Cambridge, MA: Educators Publishing Service, Inc., 1993.

―――. *A Mind at a Time.* New York: Simon & Schuster, 2002.

―――. *The Myth of Laziness.* New York: Simon & Schuster, 2004.

Lyon, G. Reid, and Norman A. Krasnegor. *Attention, Memory, and Executive Function.* Baltimore, MD: Paul H. Brookes Publishing Co., 1996.

Mooney, Jonathan, and David Cole. *Learning Outside the Lines.* New York: Fireside, 2000.

Ratey, John J. *A User's Guide to the Brain: Perception, Attention, and the Four Theaters of the Brain.* New York: Vintage Books, 2001.

Shaywitz, Sally. *Overcoming Dyslexia: A New and Complete Science-Based Program for Reading Problems at Any Level.* New York: Alfred A. Knopf, 2003.

Silver, Larry B. *The Misunderstood Child: Understanding and Coping with Your Child's Learning Disabilities.* New York: Three Rivers Press, 1998.

Smith, Sally L. *No Easy Answers: The Learning Disabled Child at Home and at School.* New York: Bantam Books, 1995.

Strauch, Barbara. *The Primal Teen: What the New Discoveries About the Teenage Brain Tell Us About Our Kids.* New York: Anchor Books, 2003.

Vail, Priscilla L. *About Dyslexia: Unraveling the Myth.* Rosemont, NJ: Modern Learning Press/Programs for Education, 1990.

———. *Smart Kids with School Problems: Things to Know and Ways to Help.* New York: Plume, 1989.

Preservation

Kovel, Ralph, and Terry Kovel. *Kovels' Quick Tips: 799 Helpful Hints on How to Care for Your Collectibles.* New York: Crown Trade Paperbacks, 1995.

Long, Jane S., and Richard W. Long (text), Ingle-Lise Eckmann (general editor). *Caring for Your Family Treasures.* New York: Harry N. Abrams, Inc., 2000.

Tuttle, Craig A. *An Ounce of Preservation: A Guide to the Care of Papers and Photographs.* Highland City, FL: Rainbow Books, Inc., 1995.

RESOURCES

Archival Supplies

Exposures
www.exposuresonline.com
800-222-4947

Light Impressions
www.lightimpressionsdirect.com
800-828-6216

Gaylord
www.gaylord.com
800-448-6160

Backpacks

L.L. Bean
www.llbean.com
800-441-5713

Jansport
www.jansport.com
Via Web site

Rocky Mountain Trail
www.rockymountaintrail.com
Various backpack brands.

Bedroom and Storage Supplies

Bed Bath & Beyond
www.bedbathandbeyond.com
800-462-3966

Crate & Barrel
www.crateandbarrel.com
800-967-6696

The Container Store
www.containerstore.com
888-266-8246

Ikea
www.ikea.com
800-434-4532

Hold Everything
www.holdeverything.com
800-421-2285

Lillian Vernon
www.lillianvernon.com
800-901-9291

Linens 'n Things
www.lnt.com
866-568-7378

Organized Living
www.organizedliving.com

Pottery Barn Teen
www.pbteen.com
866-472-4001

Target
www.target.com
800-591-3869

Techline Furniture & Cabinets
www.techlineusa.com
800-356-8400

Wal-Mart
www.walmart.com
800-925-6278

Books/Used Textbooks

When searching for used textbooks by ISBN, be sure to double-check the edition and publisher.

www.abebooks.com

www.AcademicBookServices.com

www.amazon.com

www.barnesandnoble.com

www.bigwords.com

www.eCampus.com

Disabilities

All of the following organizations have links to resources on various disabilities.

Council for Exceptional Children
www.cec.sped.org
U.S., Canada, international resources.

National Dissemination Center for Children with Disabilities
www.nichcy.org

Special Education Resources on the Internet
www.seriweb.com

Education

National Center for Education Statistics
www.nces.ed.gov

National Education Association
www.nea.org

National PTA
www.pta.org

U.S. Department of Education
www.ed.gov

School and Office Supplies

Beautone
www.beautone.com
508-634-8631

Esselte
www.esselte.com

Itoya
www.itoya.com
800-628-4811 (USA)
888-588-0345 (Canada)
0211-29-93-97 (Europe)

It's Academic
www.its-academic.com
800-454-9906

MeadWestvaco
www.mead.com

Office Depot
www.officedepot.com
800-463-3768

Office Max
www.officemax.com
800-283-7674

russell + hazel
www.russellandhazel.com
888-254-5837

Staples
www.staples.com
800-378-2753

Viking Office Products
www.viking.com
800-711-4242

Specialty Items

The Organized Student
www.organizedstudent.com

Franklin Electronic Publishers, Inc.
www.franklin.com
800-266-5626

Inspiration
www.inspiration.com
800-877-4292
Software tools to develop ideas and organize thinking.

Red Dot, Inc.
503-598-0990
A unique organizer for filing school papers from preschool
to twelfth grade.

Schoolfolio
www.schoolfolio.com
800-288-4195
A very large storage box that organizes keepsakes from
preschool to twelfth grade.

Time Timer
www.timetimer.com
877-771-8463

Free Helpful Web Sites

Epinions
www.epinions.com
Thirty categories of products and services reviewed by
consumers.

CNETNetworks
www.cnetnetworks.com
Global companies inform consumers about technology,
games, entertainment, and business technology.

Consumer Search
www.consumersearch.com
Categories reviewed: electronics, house/home, auto, computers, kitchen, health/fitness, photo/video, family, sports/leisure, office, personal finance, lawn/garden.

Price Grabber
www.pricegrabber.com
Information regarding products: specifications, descriptions, ratings, and price comparisons. Categories include: computers, photo, electronics, home & garden, movies, video games, toys, jewelry & watches, babies & kids, health & beauty.

SHOPPING LIST

GENERAL

- ☐ colored markers
- ☐ label maker
- ☐ label maker tape

THE BACKPACK AND LOCKER

- ☐ backpack
- ☐ backpack accessories
  - ☐ cellphone holder
  - ☐ keychain, extra keys
  - ☐ general information sheet
- ☐ locker accessories
  - ☐ extra shelf
  - ☐ message board
  - ☐ pad and pen

TRAVELING PAPER

- ☐ accordion file
  - ☐ 7 pocket
  - ☐ 13 pocket
- ☐ 3-hole punched lined pad
- ☐ subject notebooks
  - ☐ composition
  - ☐ graph paper
  - ☐ spiral
  - ☐ wireless
- ☐ 3-ring binders:
  - ☐ ½ inch
  - ☐ 1 inch
  - ☐ 1½ inch
- ☐ paper
  - ☐ 3-hole punched
  - ☐ graph paper
- ☐ pencil case
- ☐ poly dividers
- ☐ poly pocket folders

DESKTOP FILING SYSTEM

- ☐ desktop file box
- ☐ hanging files with tabs and inserts

THE DESK AND PORTABLE OFFICE

☐ art/tackle box
☐ book covers
☐ bulletin board and push pins
☐ calculator
☐ calendar
☐ colored pencils
☐ compass
☐ correction fluid/pen/tape
☐ desk
☐ desk accessories
☐ desk chair
☐ desk lamp
☐ drawer organizer(s)
☐ glue
☐ highlighter(s)
☐ index cards and holders
☐ letter tray(s)
☐ lined pad(s)
☐ markers
☐ paper clips
☐ paper:
   ☐ colored
   ☐ construction
   ☐ loose-leaf
   ☐ reinforced loose-leaf
☐ pencil sharpener
☐ pencils
☐ pens
☐ protractor(s)
☐ reference books
   ☐ dictionary
   ☐ thesaurus
☐ reinforcements
☐ report covers
☐ rubber bands
☐ ruler(s)
☐ scissors
☐ self-stick notes
☐ stapler and staples
☐ tape
☐ 3-hole punch

COMPUTER SUPPLIES

- ☐ adjustable chair
- ☐ CD disc holder
- ☐ computer
- ☐ computer desk
- ☐ computer disc holder
- ☐ computer discs
- ☐ computer paper
- ☐ ink cartridges
- ☐ printer
- ☐ printer paper

TIME MANAGEMENT

- ☐ analog clock
- ☐ analog watch
- ☐ teacher's plan book
- ☐ self-stick flags
- ☐ calendar(s)
  - ☐ 8½" x 11" (monthly)
- ☐ monthly (household)
- ☐ weekly (household)

END-OF-YEAR WRAP-UP

- ☐ accordion file or hanging file
- ☐ archival box(es)
- ☐ poly envelope
- ☐ portfolio

FOR THE ROOM

- ☐ magazine holder
- ☐ storage boxes
- ☐ storage for toiletries
- ☐ wastebasket

ABOUT THE AUTHORS

DONNA GOLDBERG is founder and director of the Organized Student. She started her consulting business while working as a librarian at the Dalton School in New York. In addition to her individualized consulting work, Mrs. Goldberg presents public seminars and speeches to organizations, schools, and business groups. She has been featured on CNN, CNBC and *Good Morning America,* as well as in *The New York Times, The Wall Street Journal, Los Angeles Times, San Francisco Chronicle,* and several national publications. Mrs. Goldberg lives in New York with her husband, Jack, and is the mother of two sons, Noah and Saul.

JENNIFER ZWIEBEL is a coach, organizer, and writer. Ms. Zwiebel worked as a clinician at Lindamood-Bell Learning Processes before becoming an organizing consultant. In 2002, she joined Mrs. Goldberg at the Organized Student and continues to work with students of all ages. A graduate of Brown University, Ms. Zwiebel lives in New York with her husband, Matt.